Color With Your Besties
Sherri Baldy
Coloring Books

About The Artist

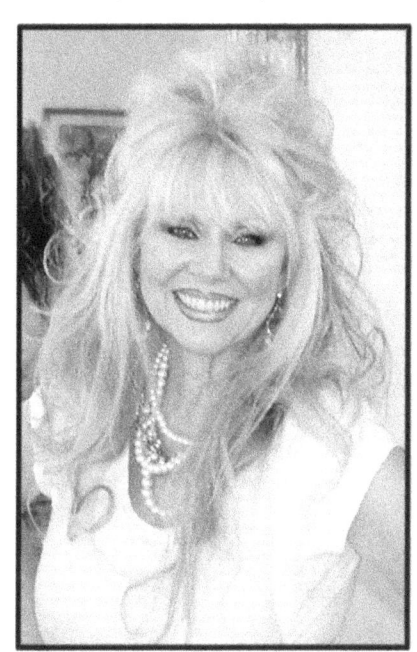

Sherri Baldy is known for her trademark Big Eyed art for over 20 plus years around the world. She is a multi media artist that is licensed on a wide range of products. Sherri lives in Riverside, Calif. with her husband on their farm (Urban Farm Diva Farms) She has two sons Kyler & Josh & two daughter Courtney & Brittany.

When she is not painting, drawing and creating craft products for the craft industry, she spends her time in the gardens at the farm and in her "Barn Studio" that is open to the public by appointment.
Sherri Baldy is now offering her Big Eyed My-Bestie artwork in coloring books.
These fun coloring books come with 2 copies of each image for you to color, or better yet, have a Bestie party and color with one of your Besties Pals or keep them all to yourself :-)
Most of all have FUN, Color, Relax and Enjoy!

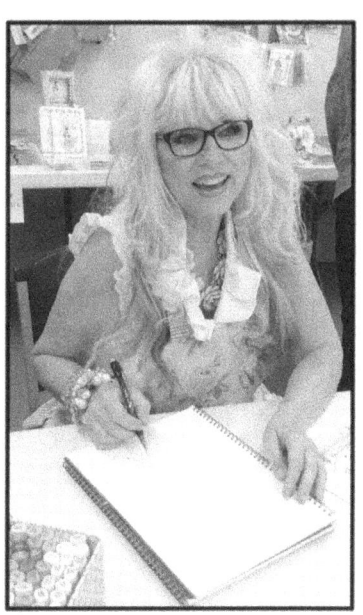

www.MyBestiesShop.com
Sherri Baldy My Besties Coloring Books in Riverside CA.
Copyright Sherri Baldy ~ My-Besties TM

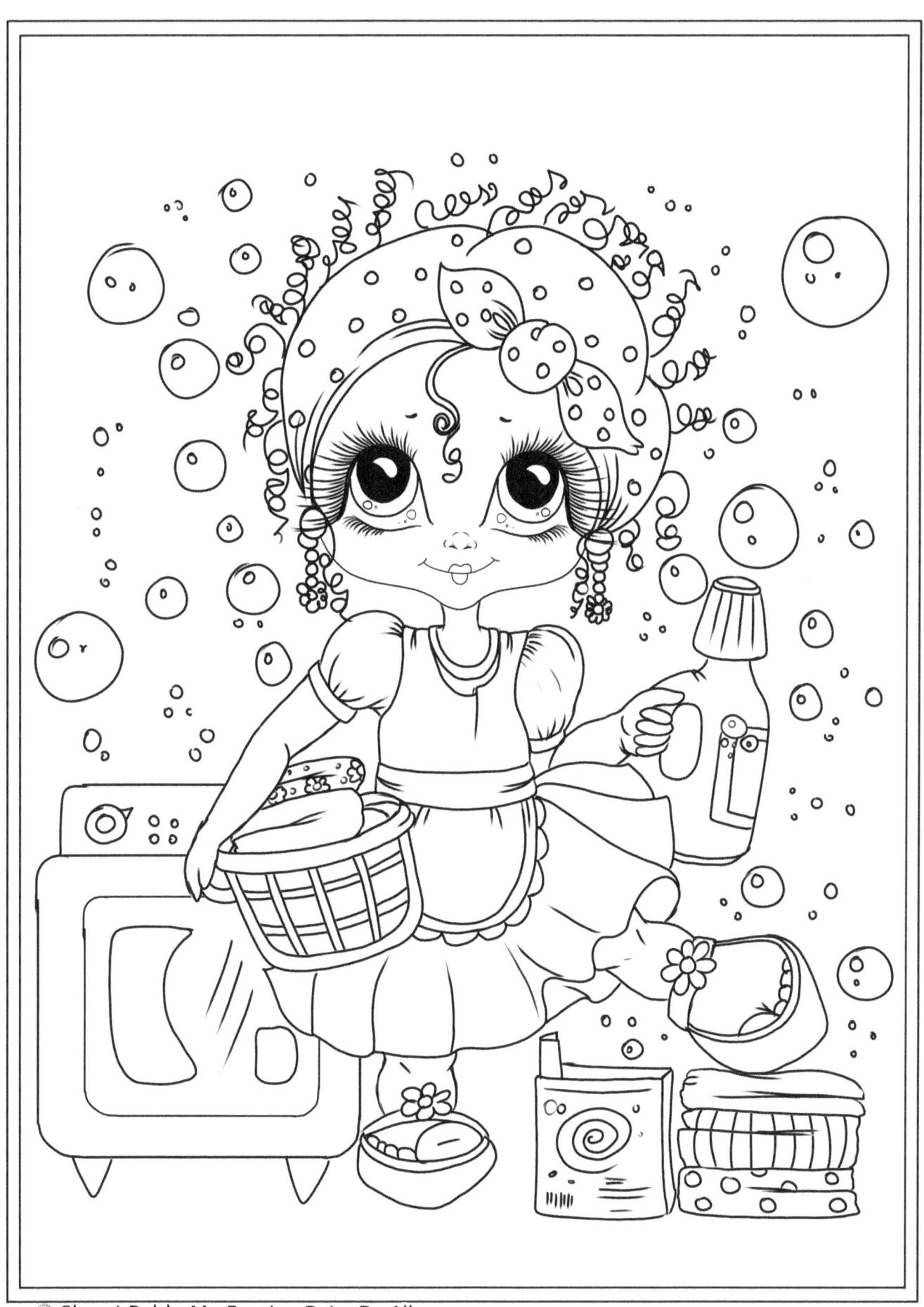

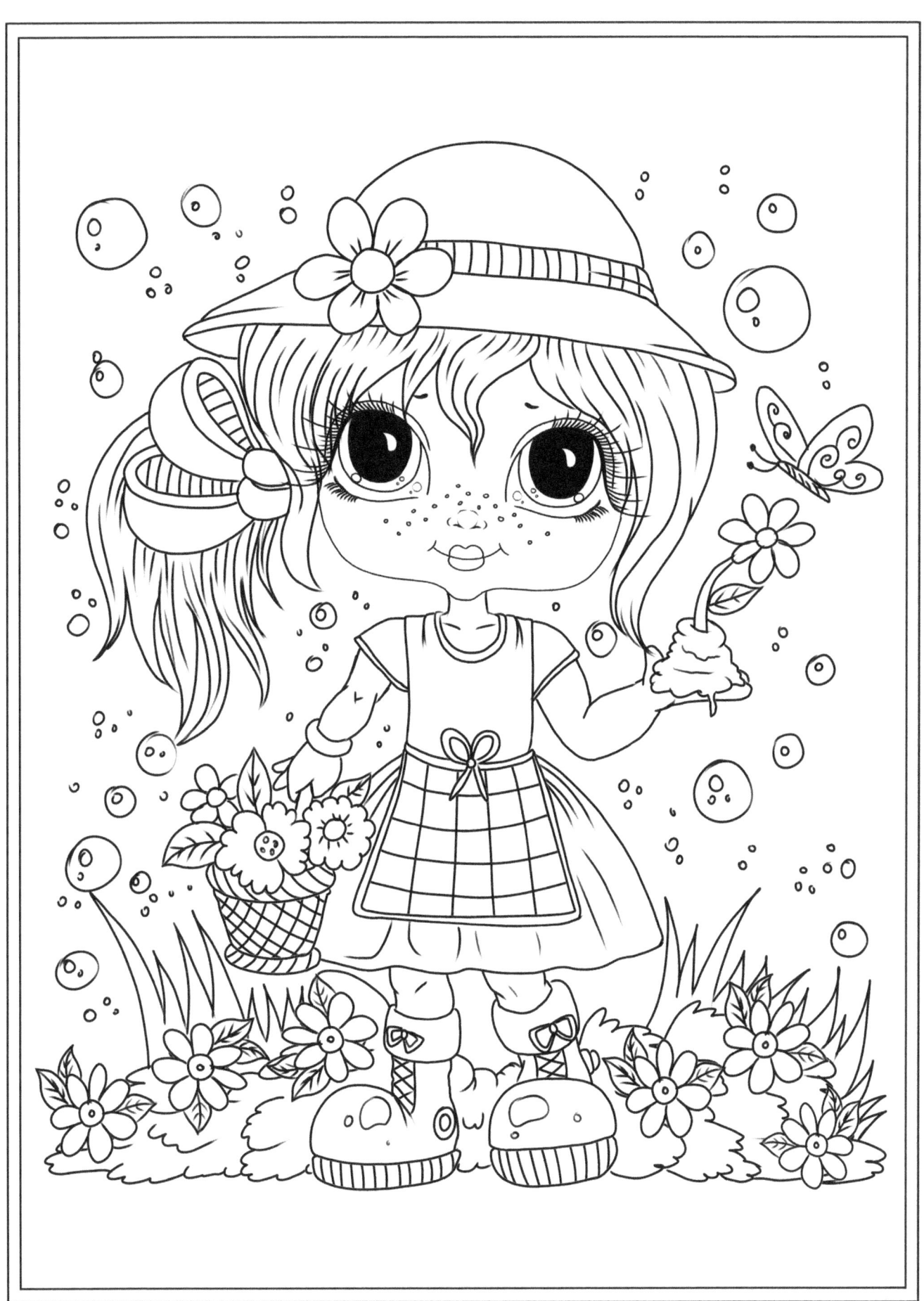

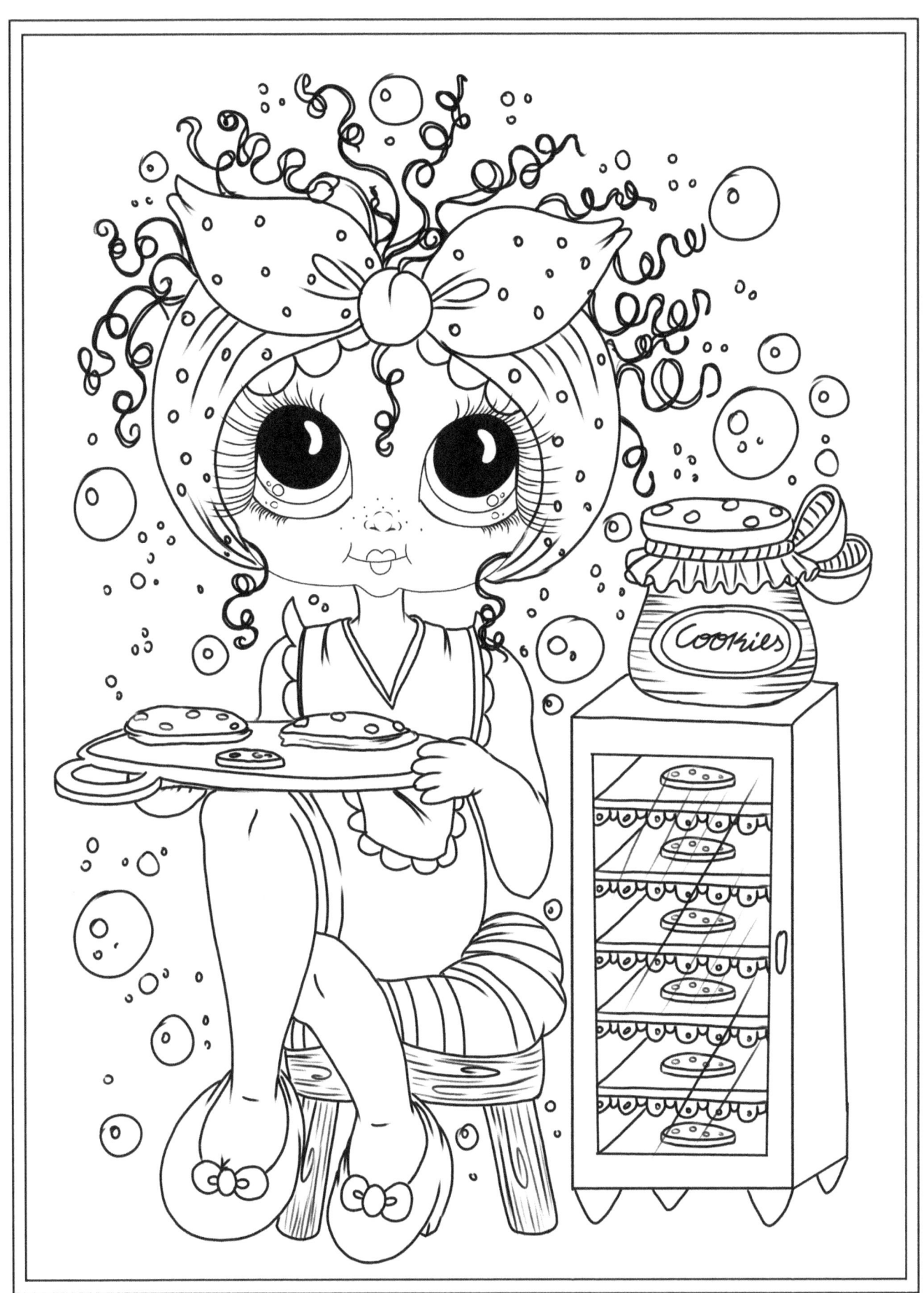

© Sherri Baldy My-Besties Daisy Do All

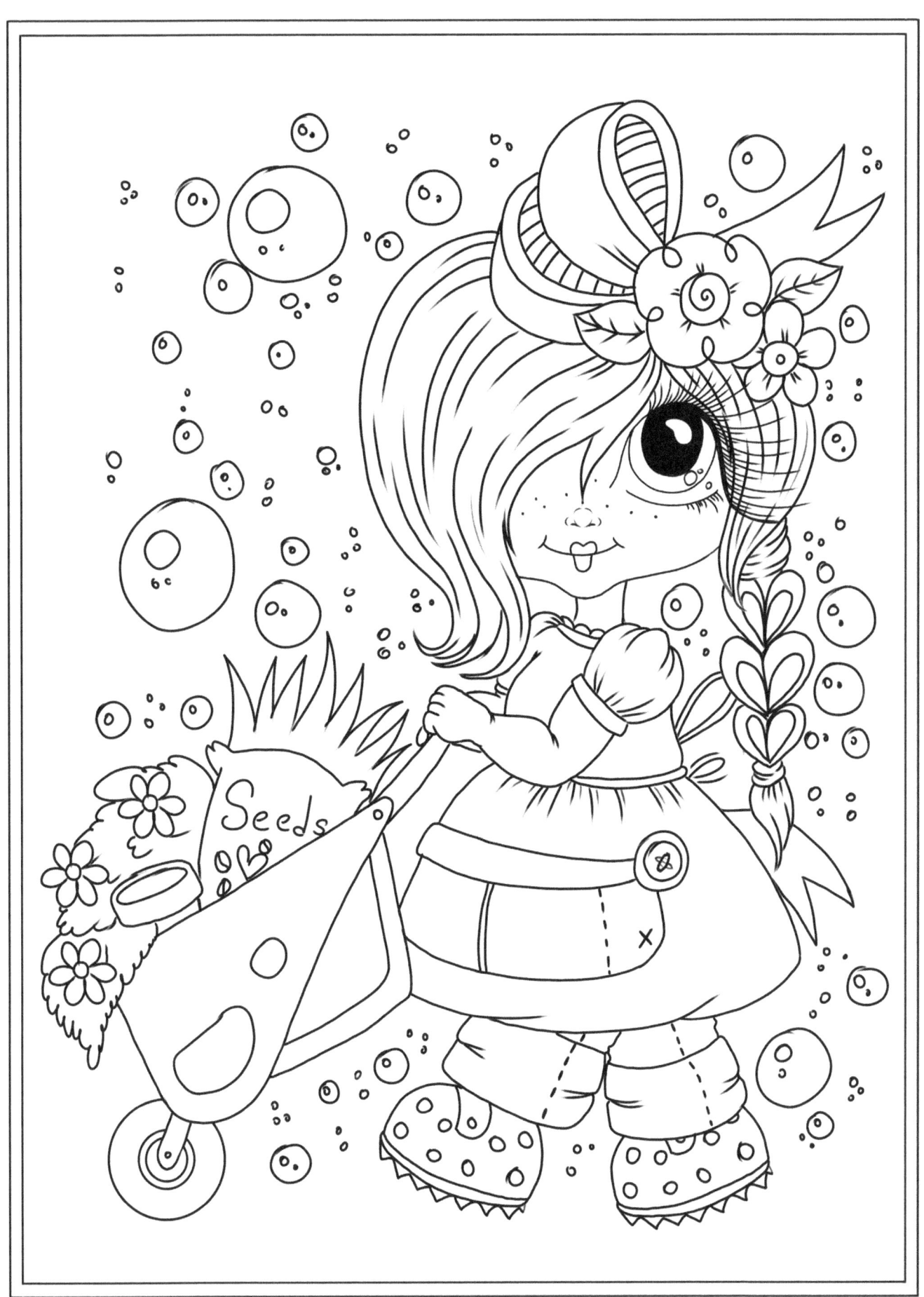

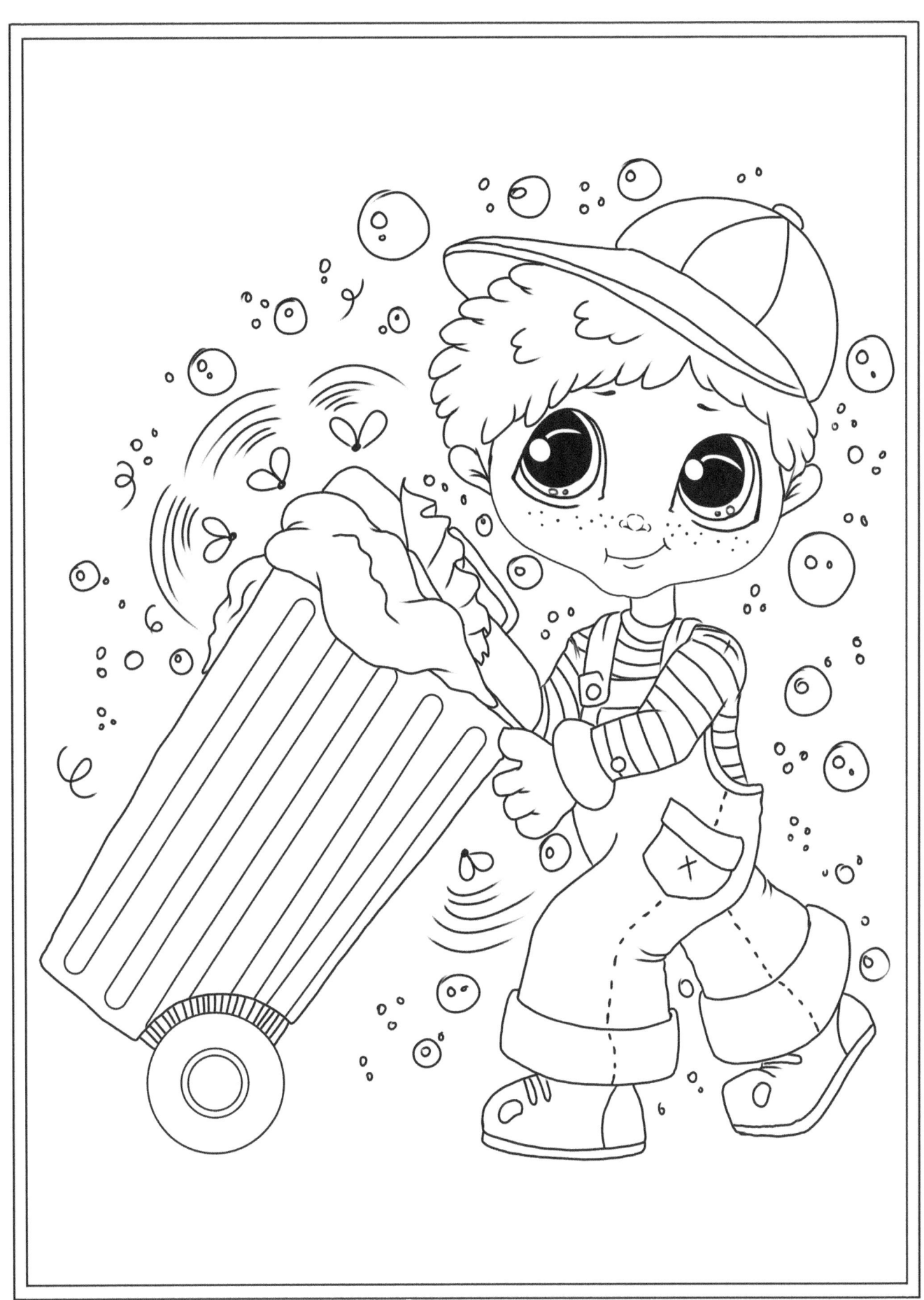

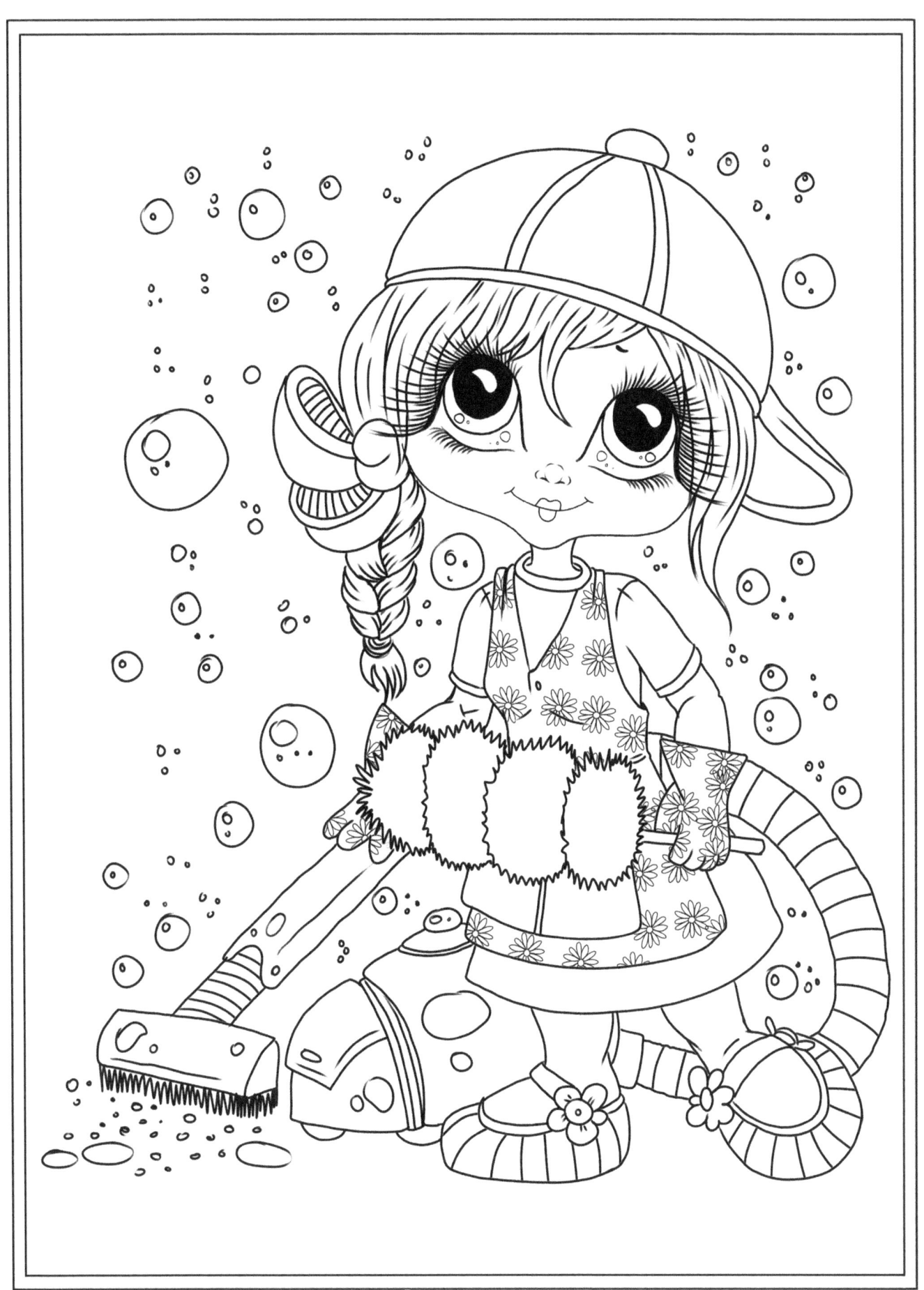

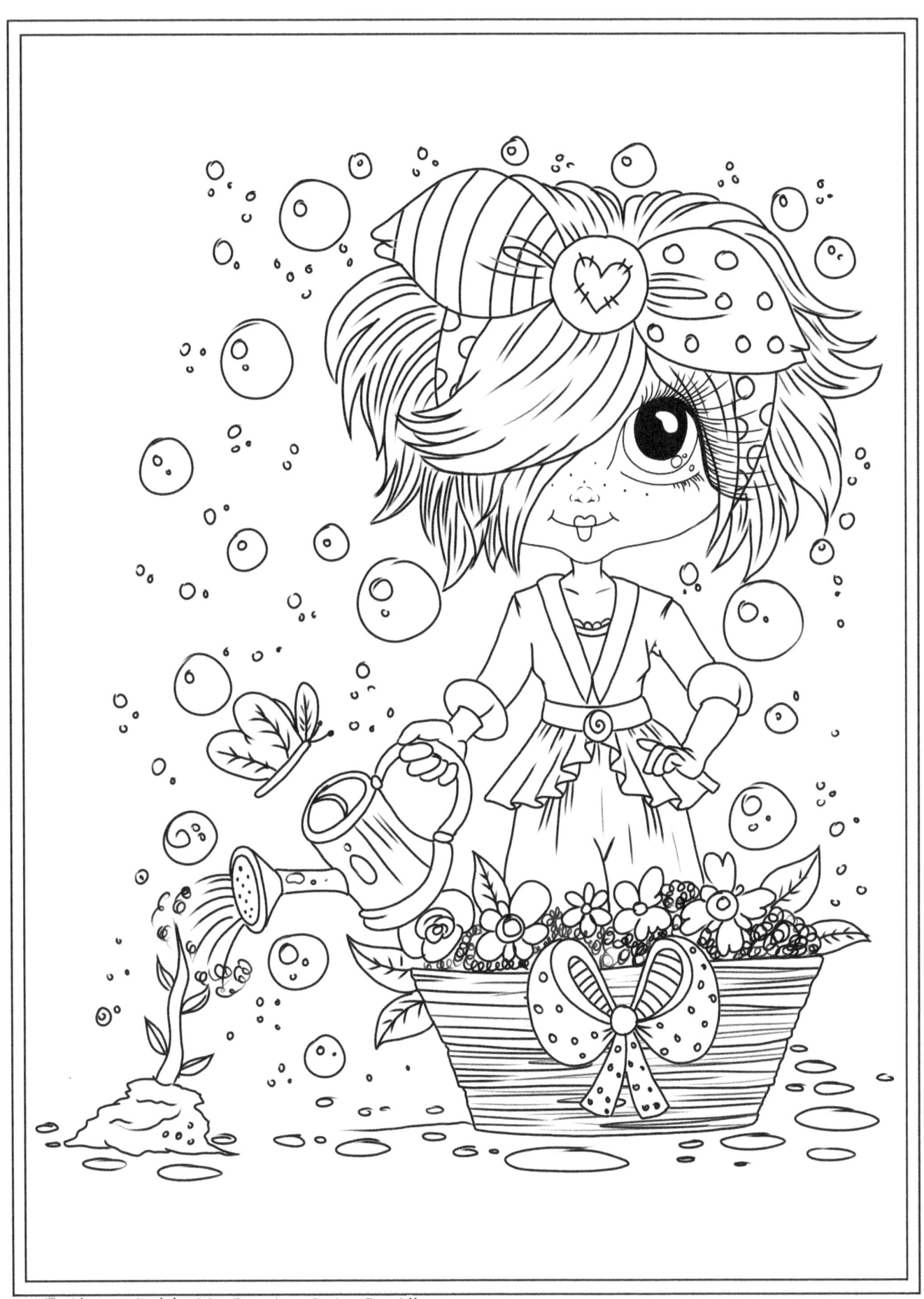

© Sherri Baldy My-Besties Daisy Do All

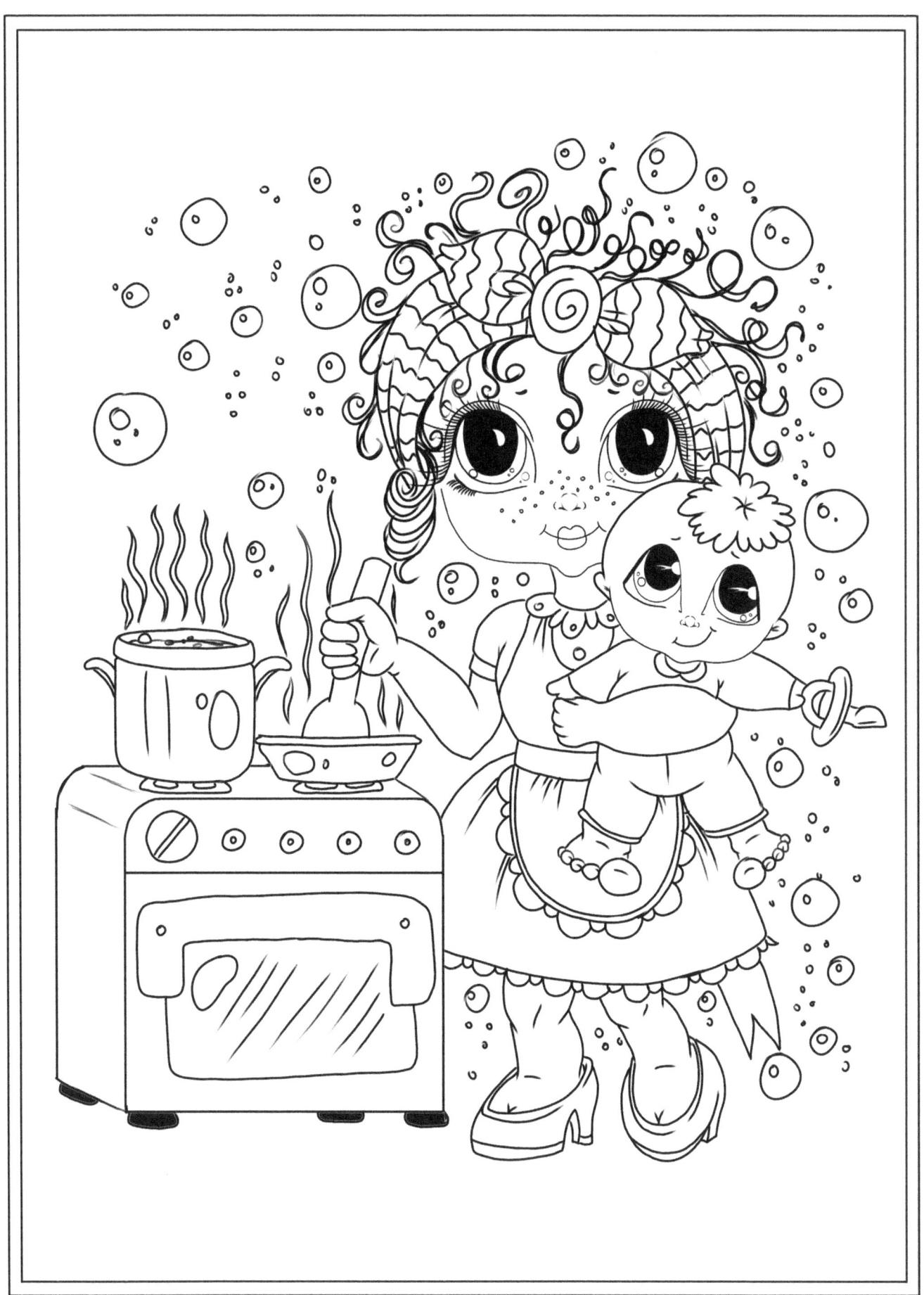

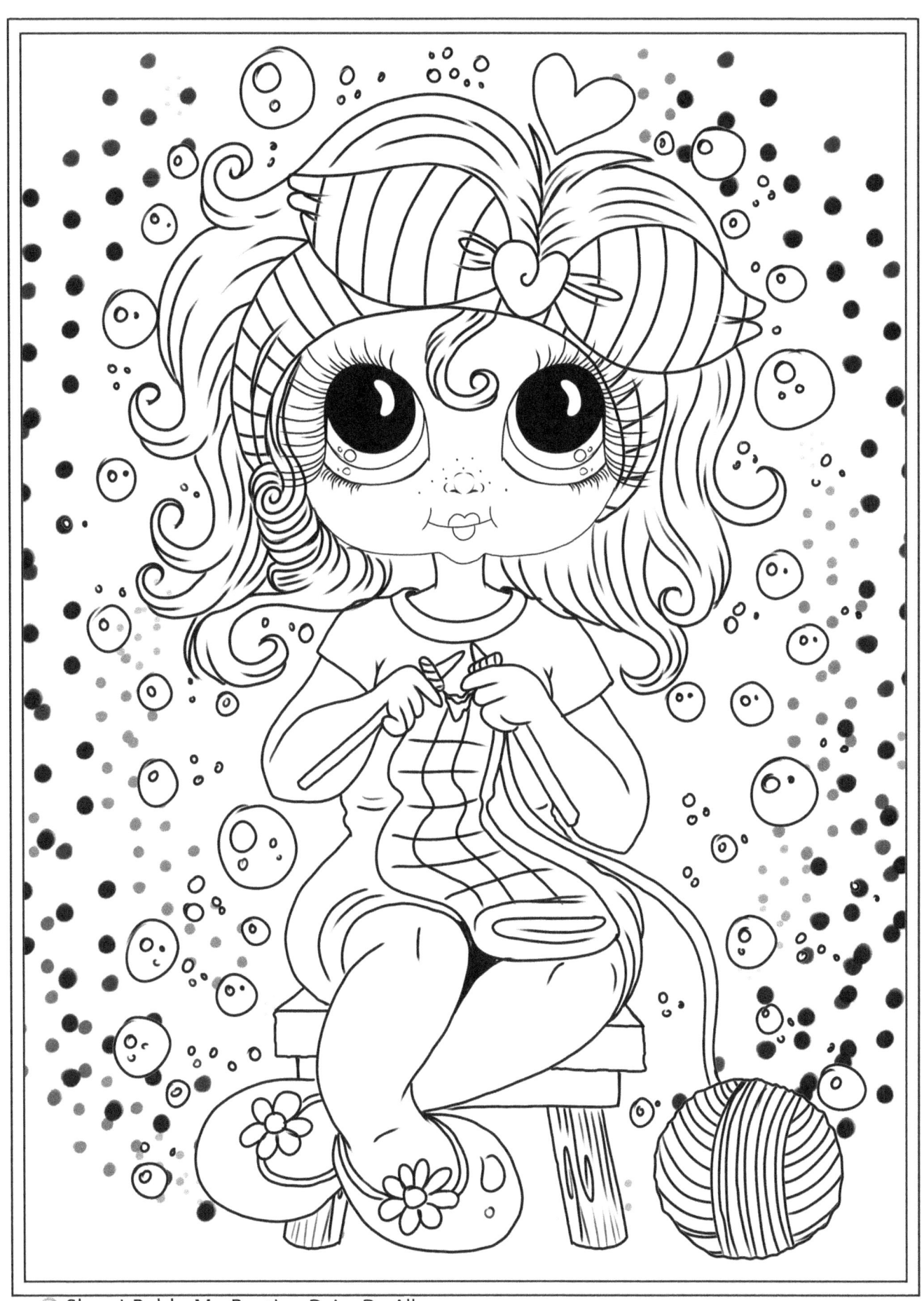

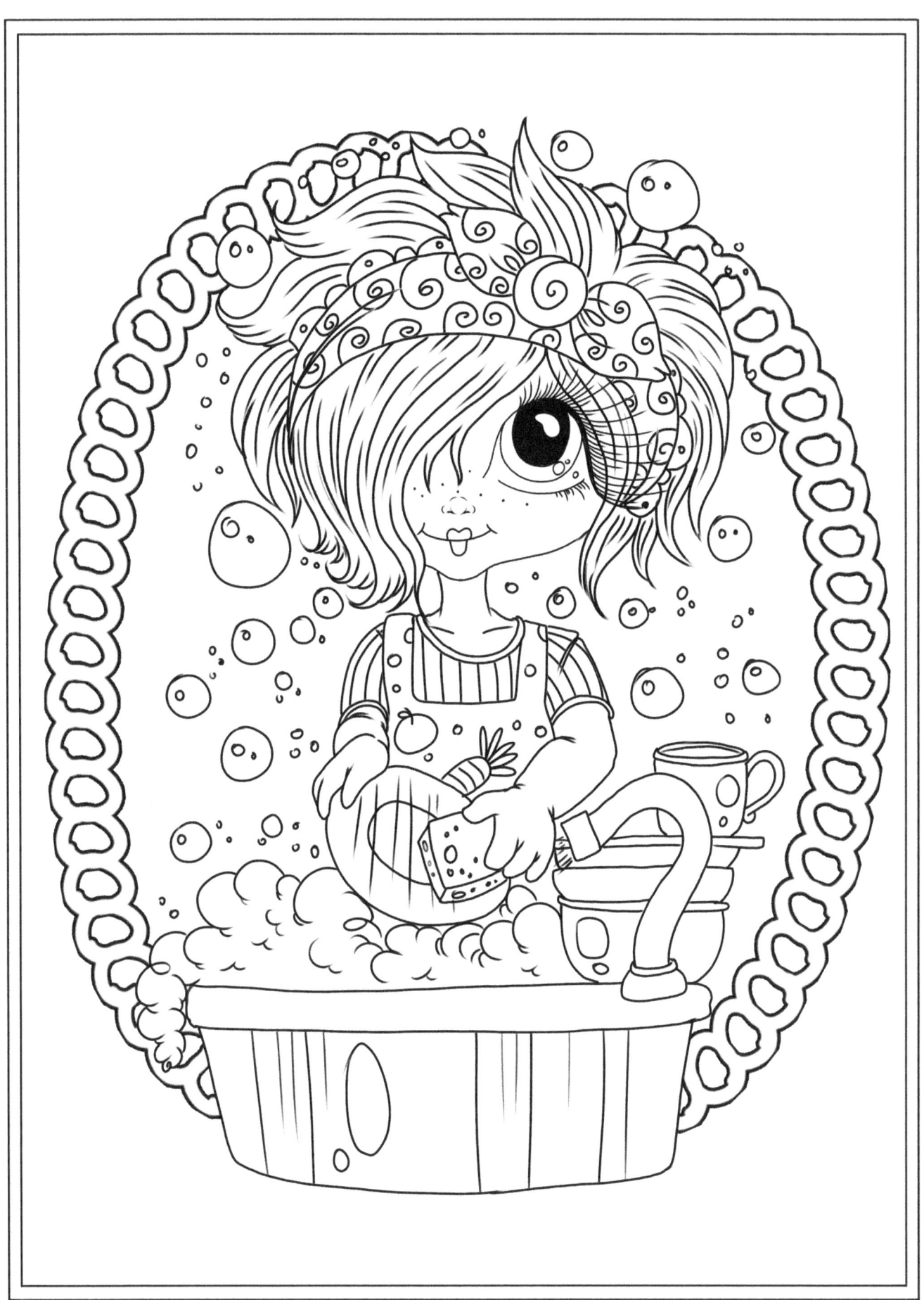

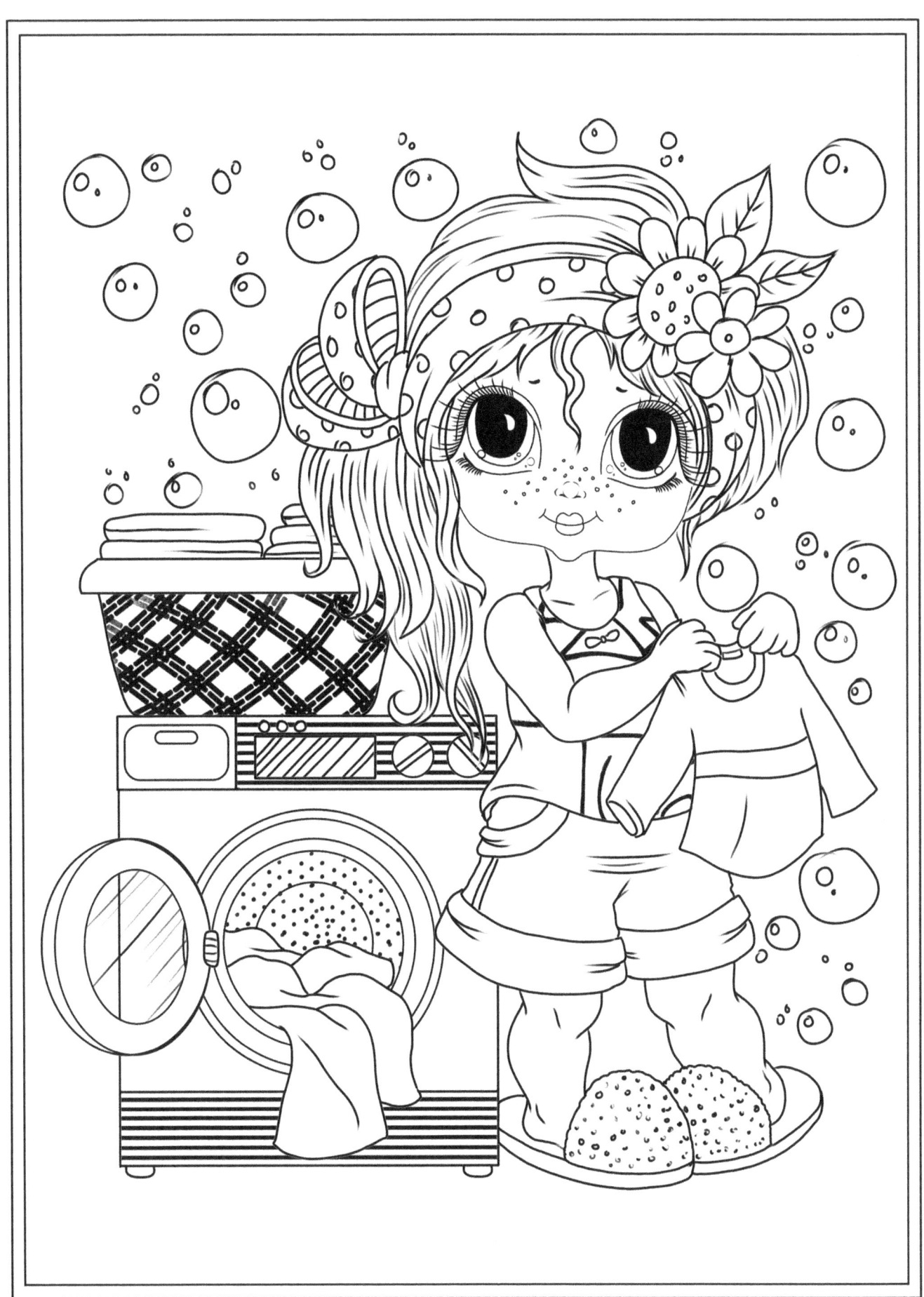

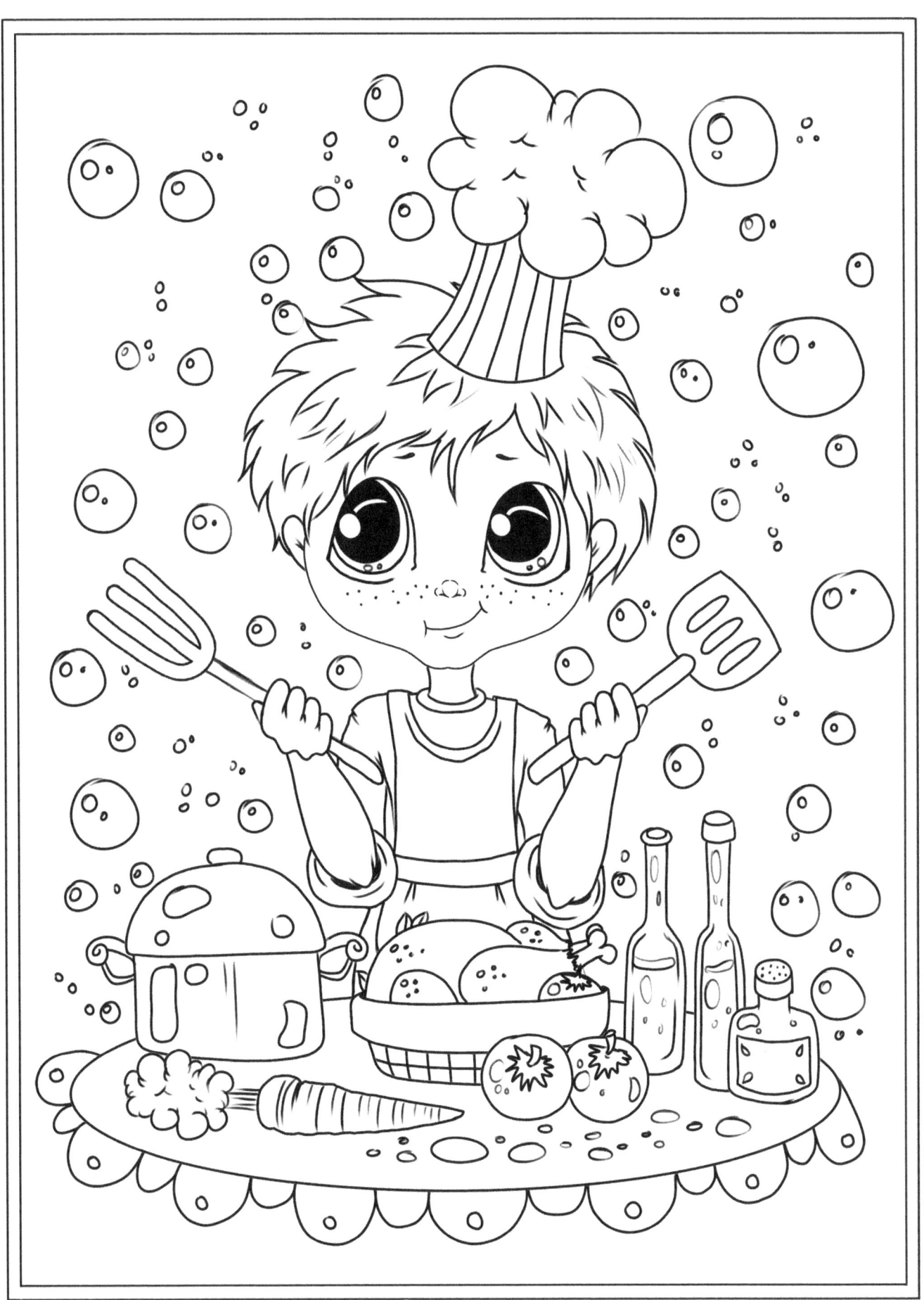

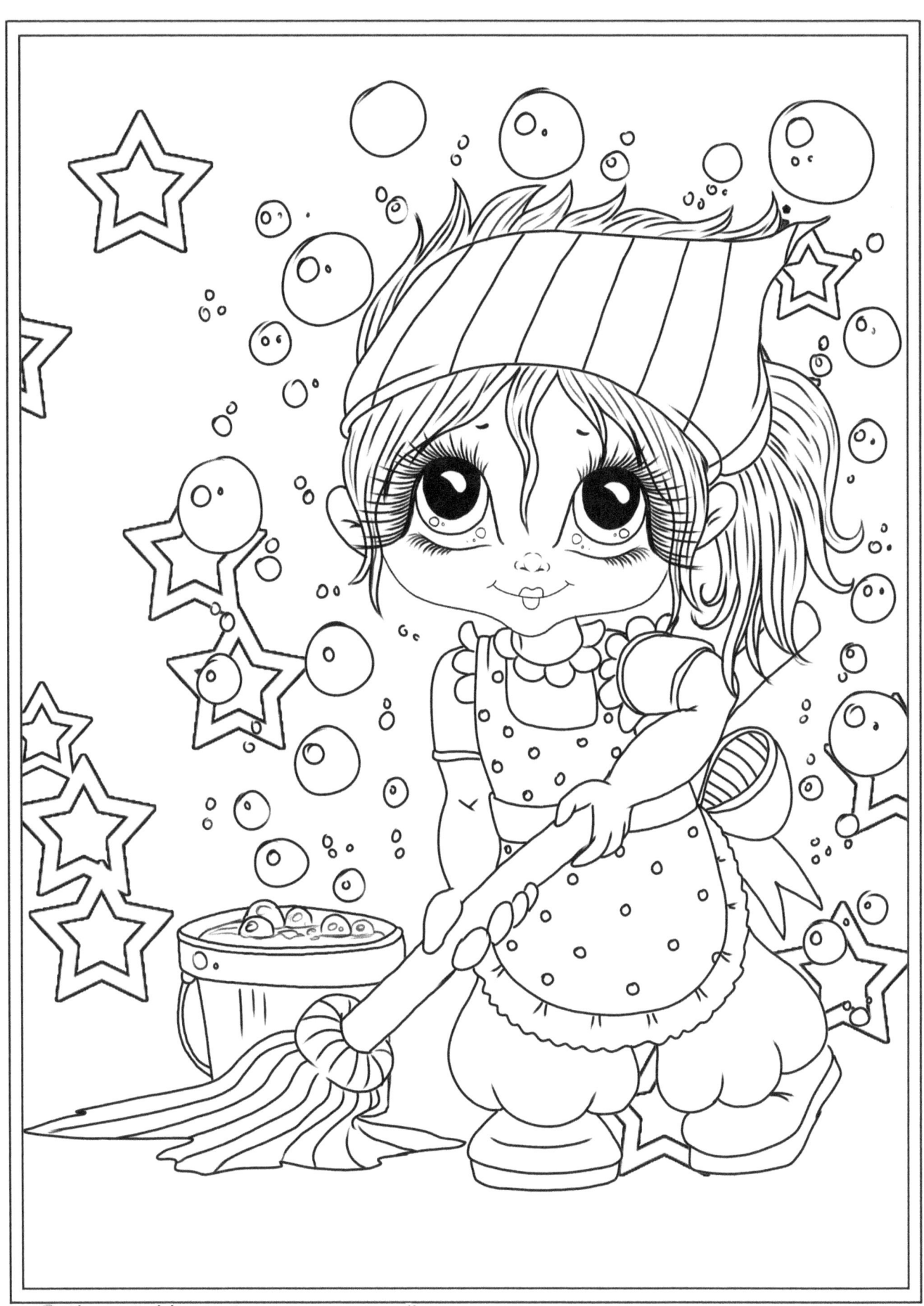

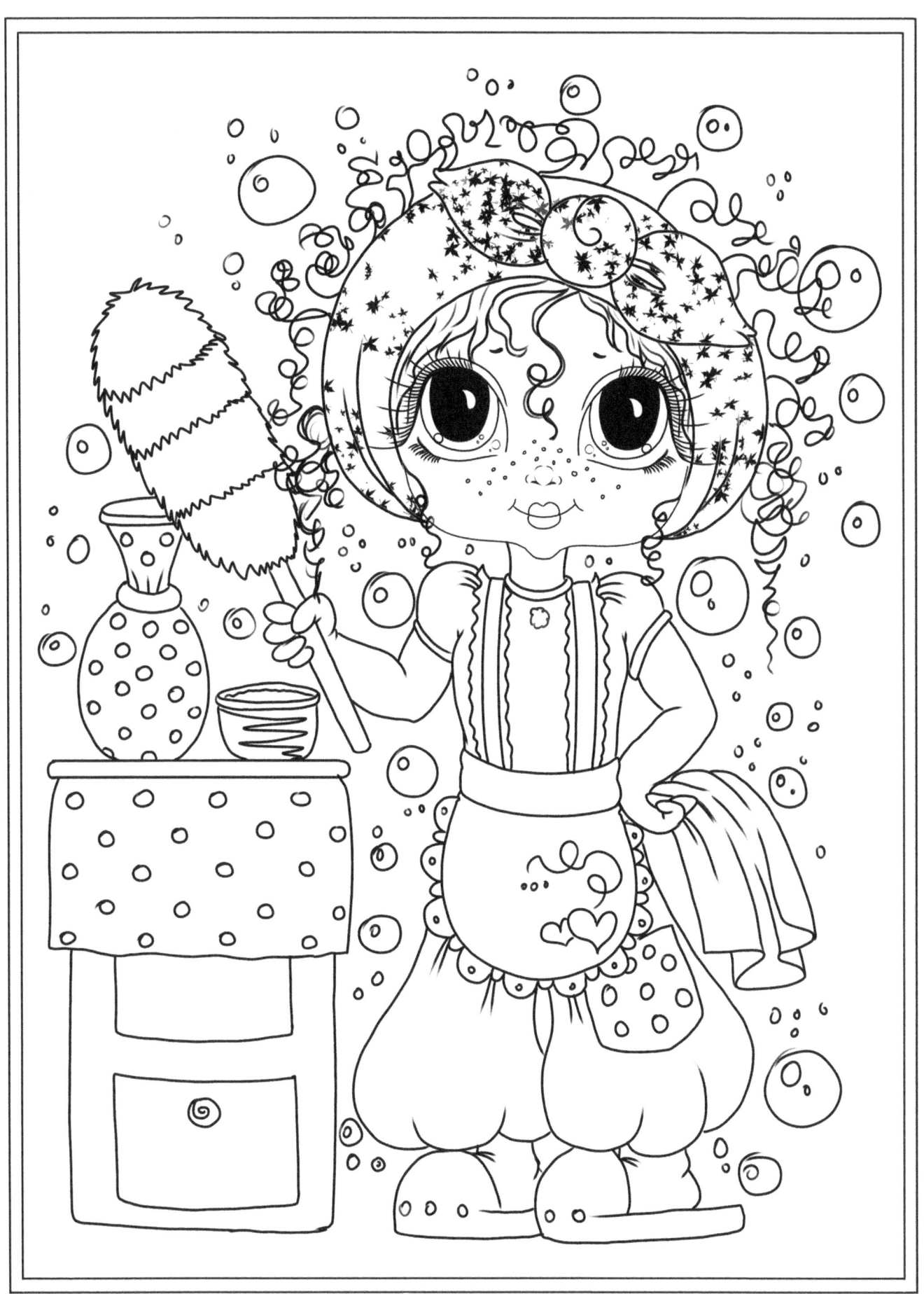

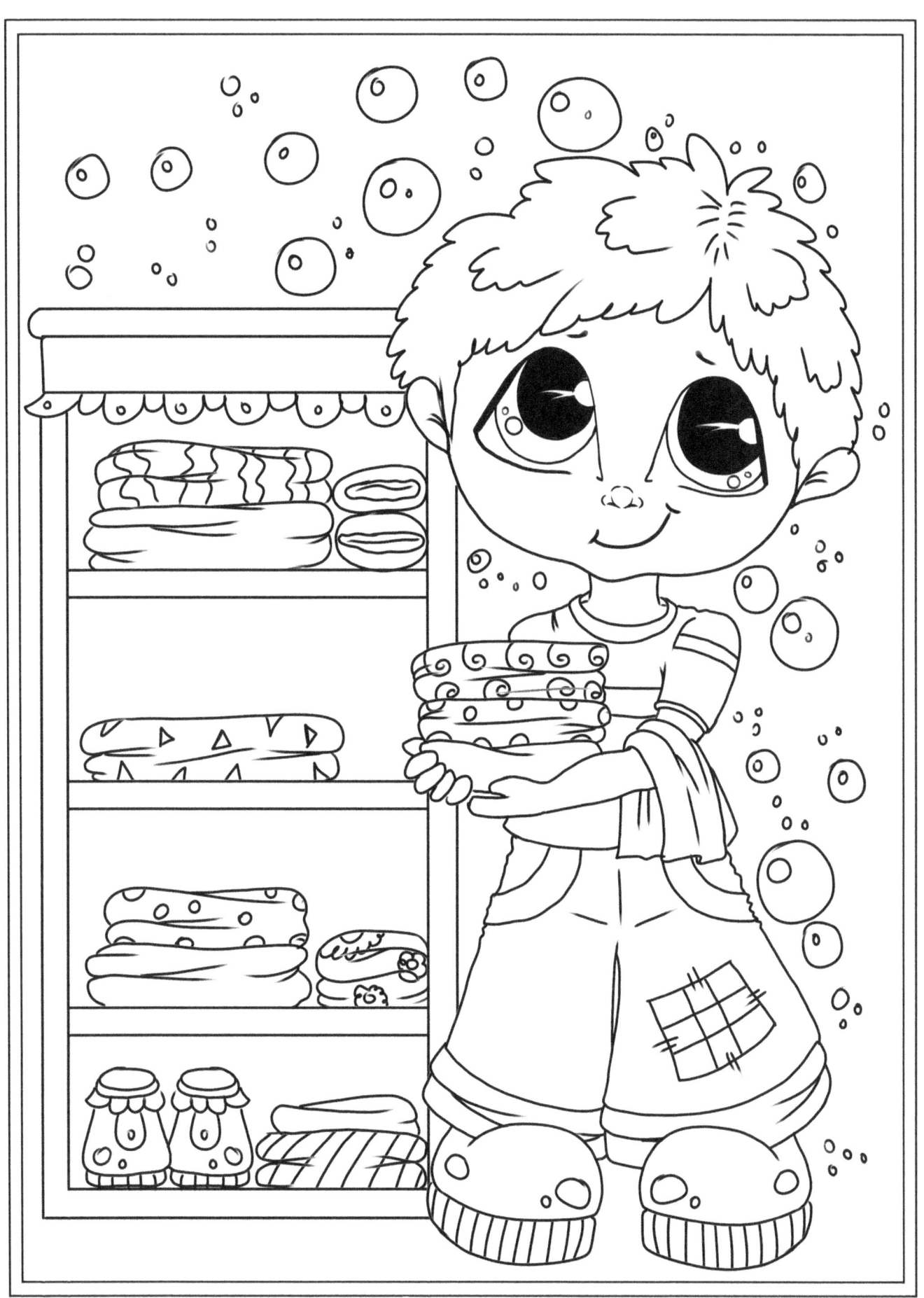

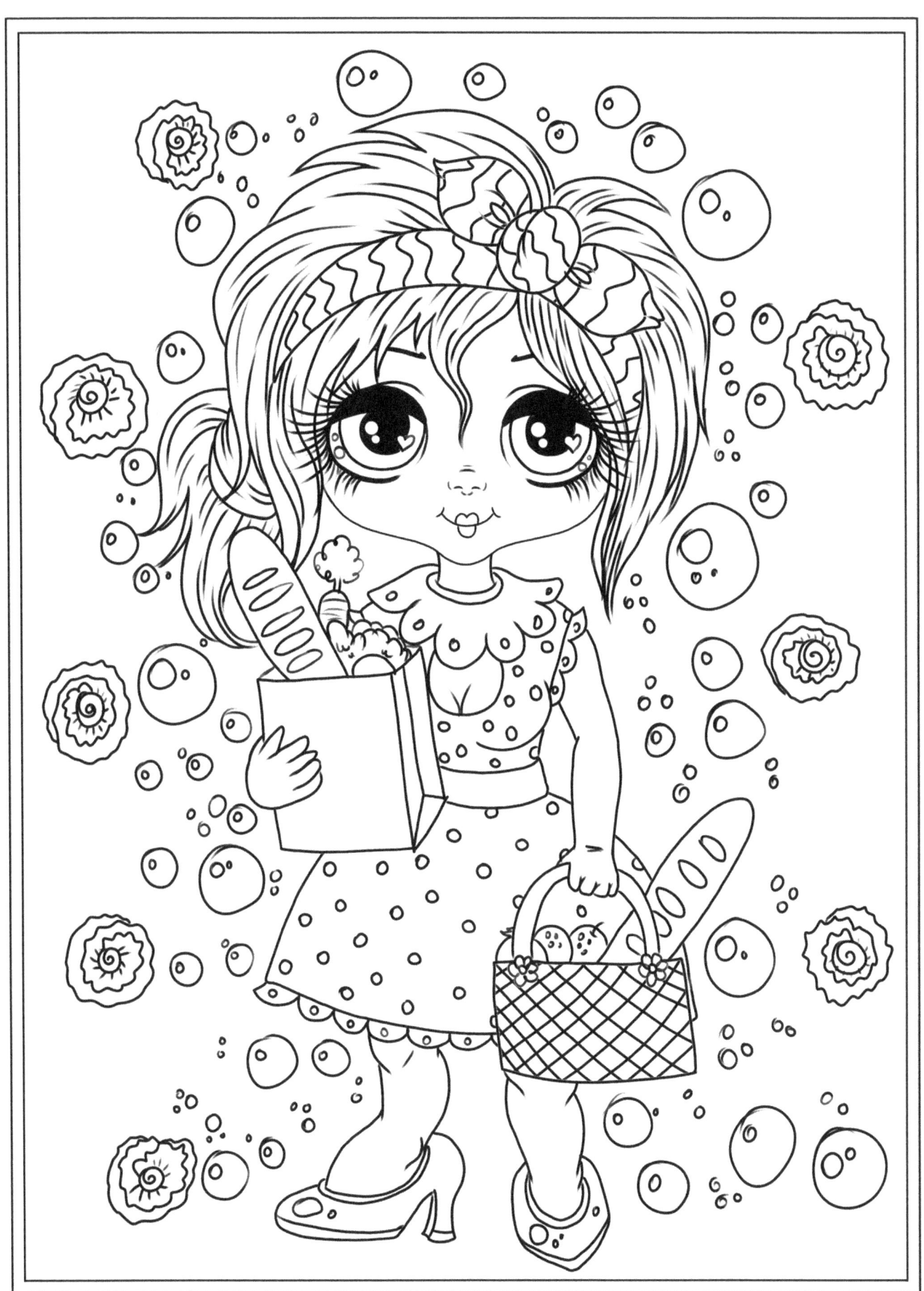

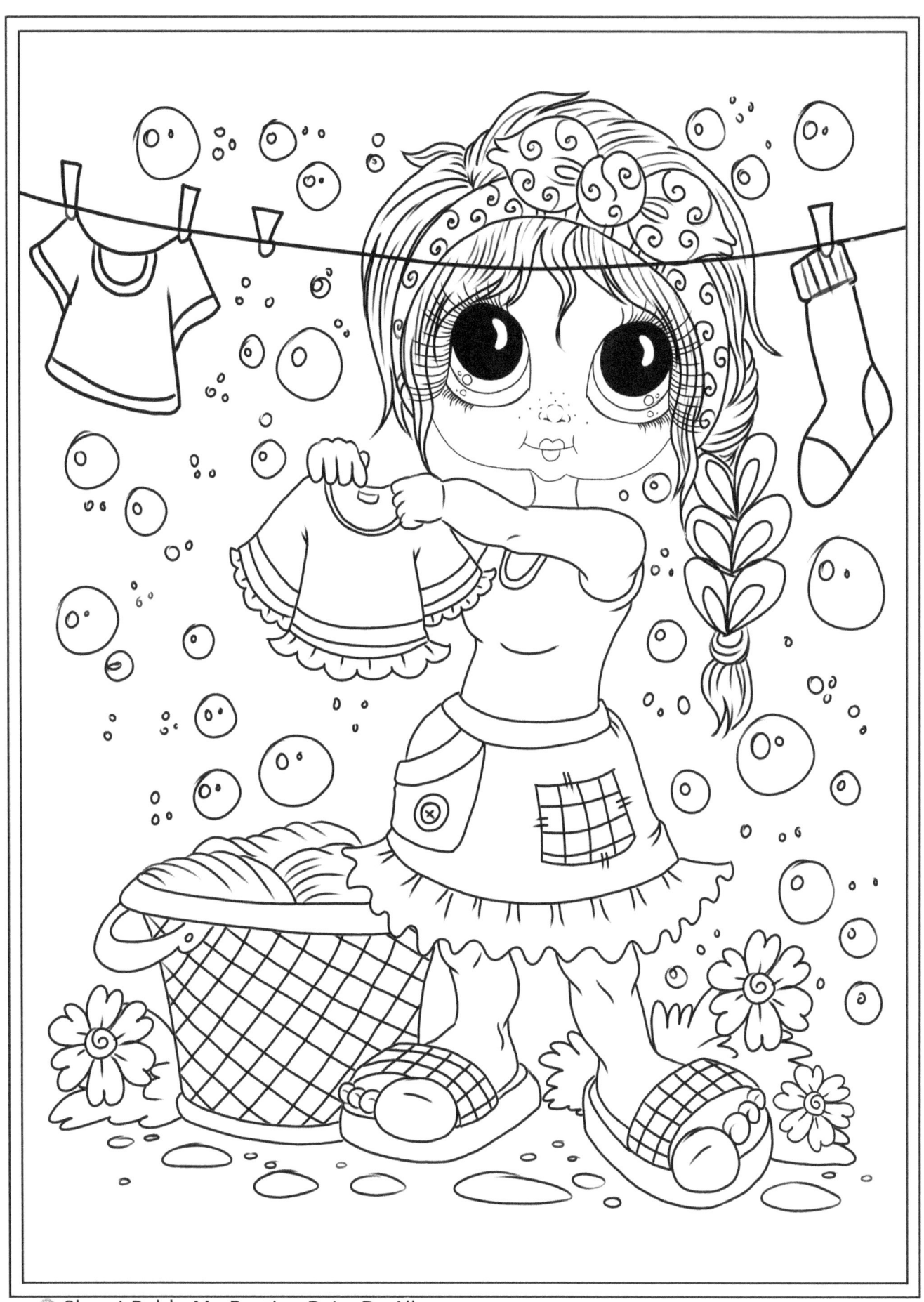

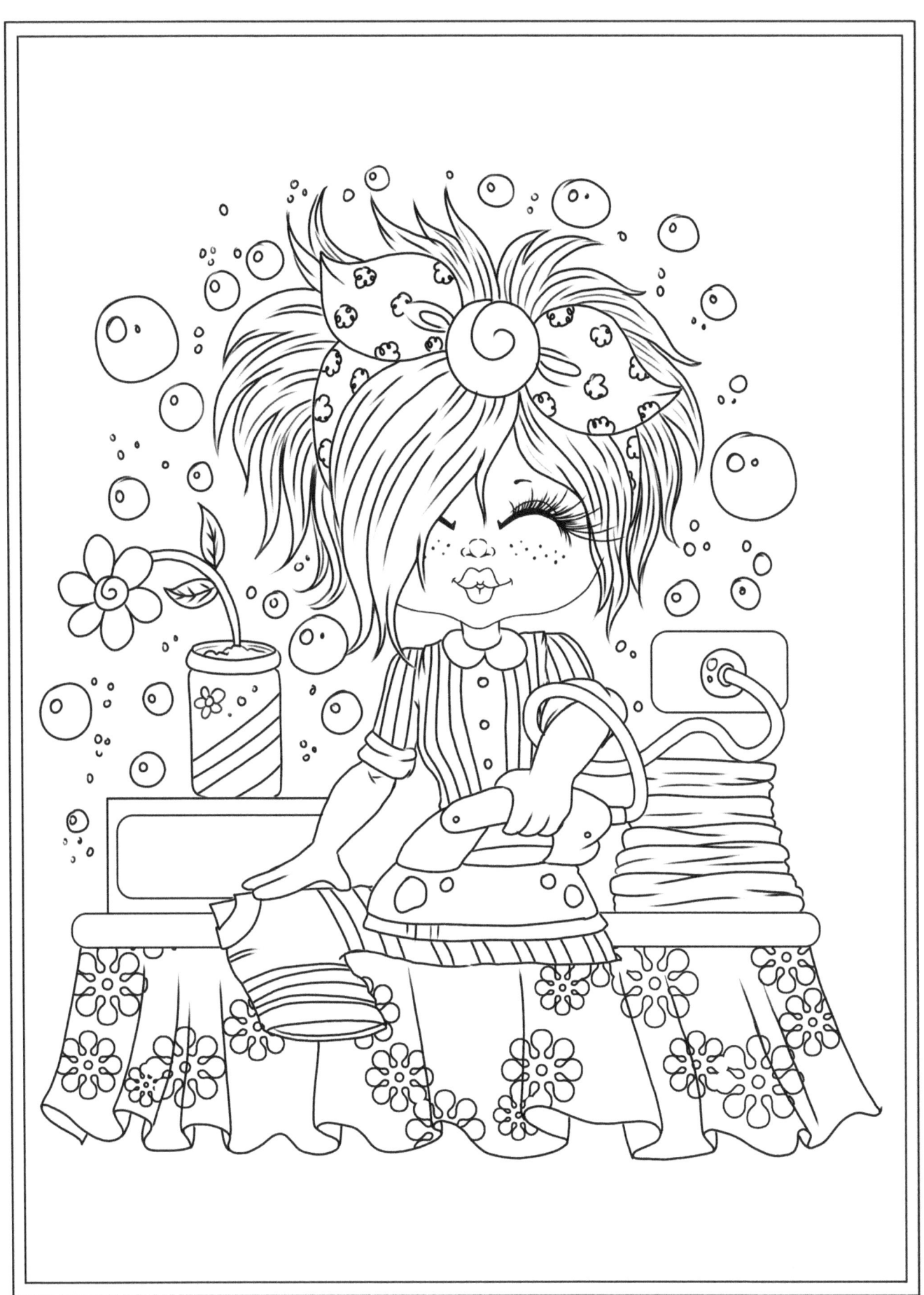

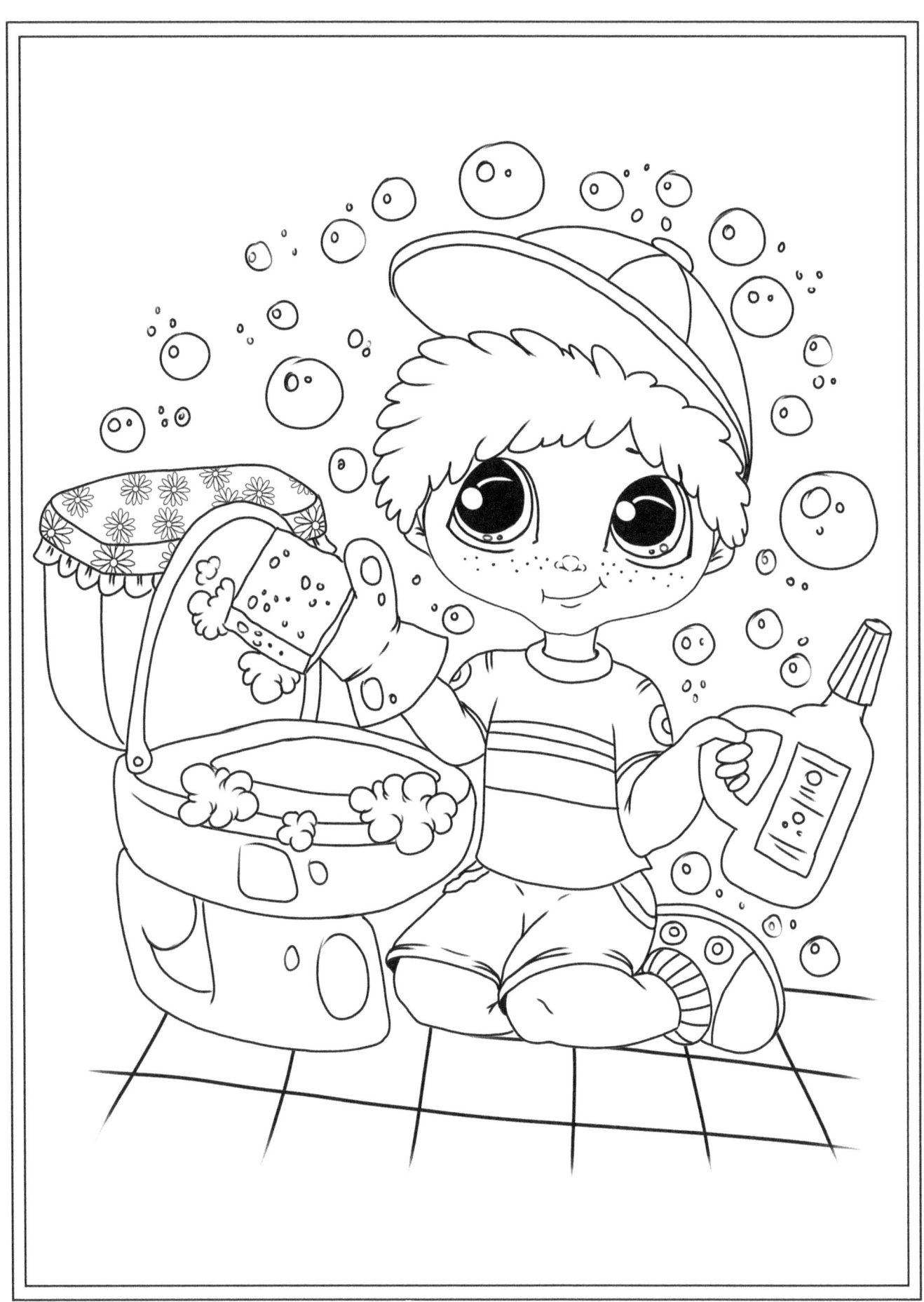

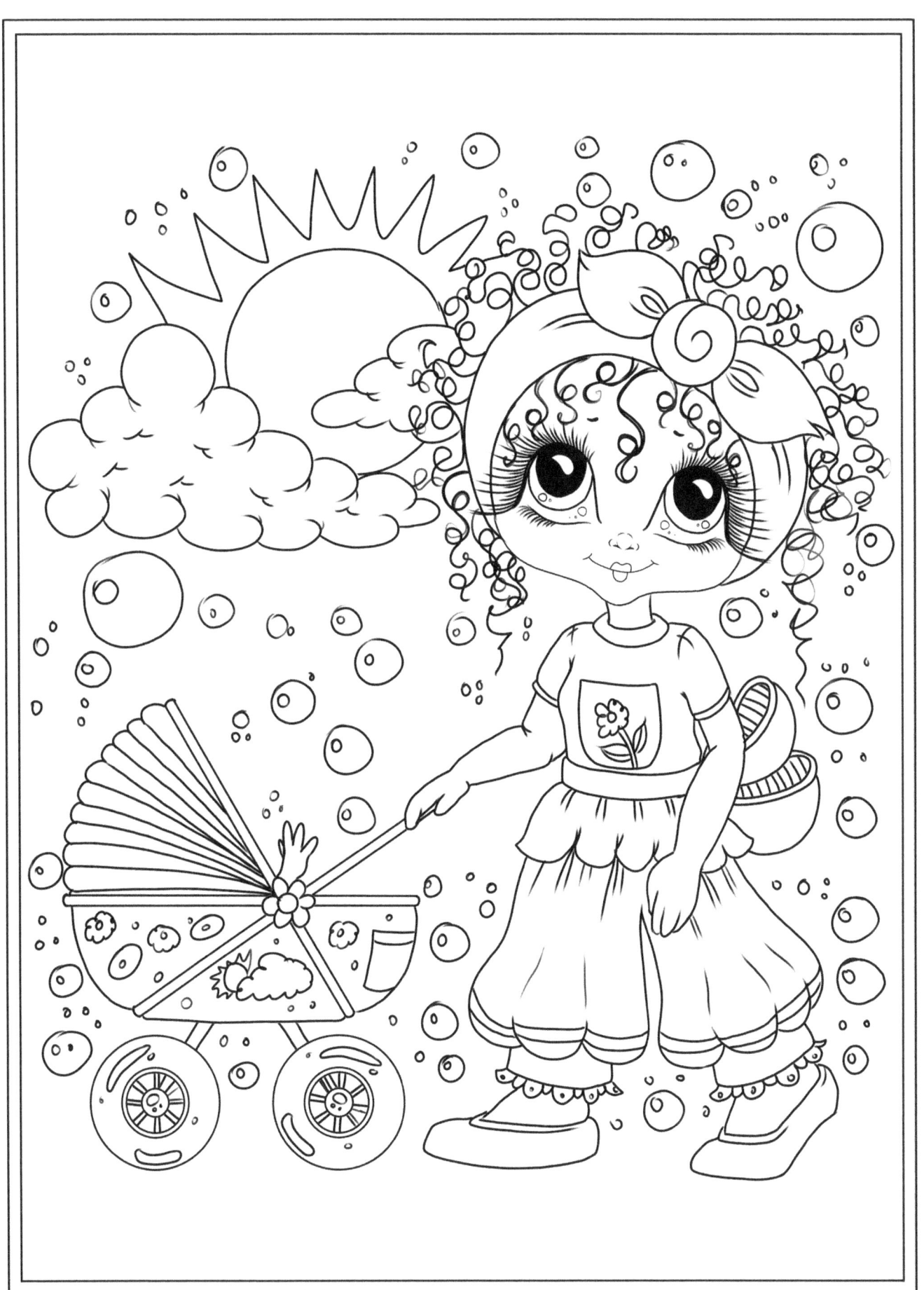

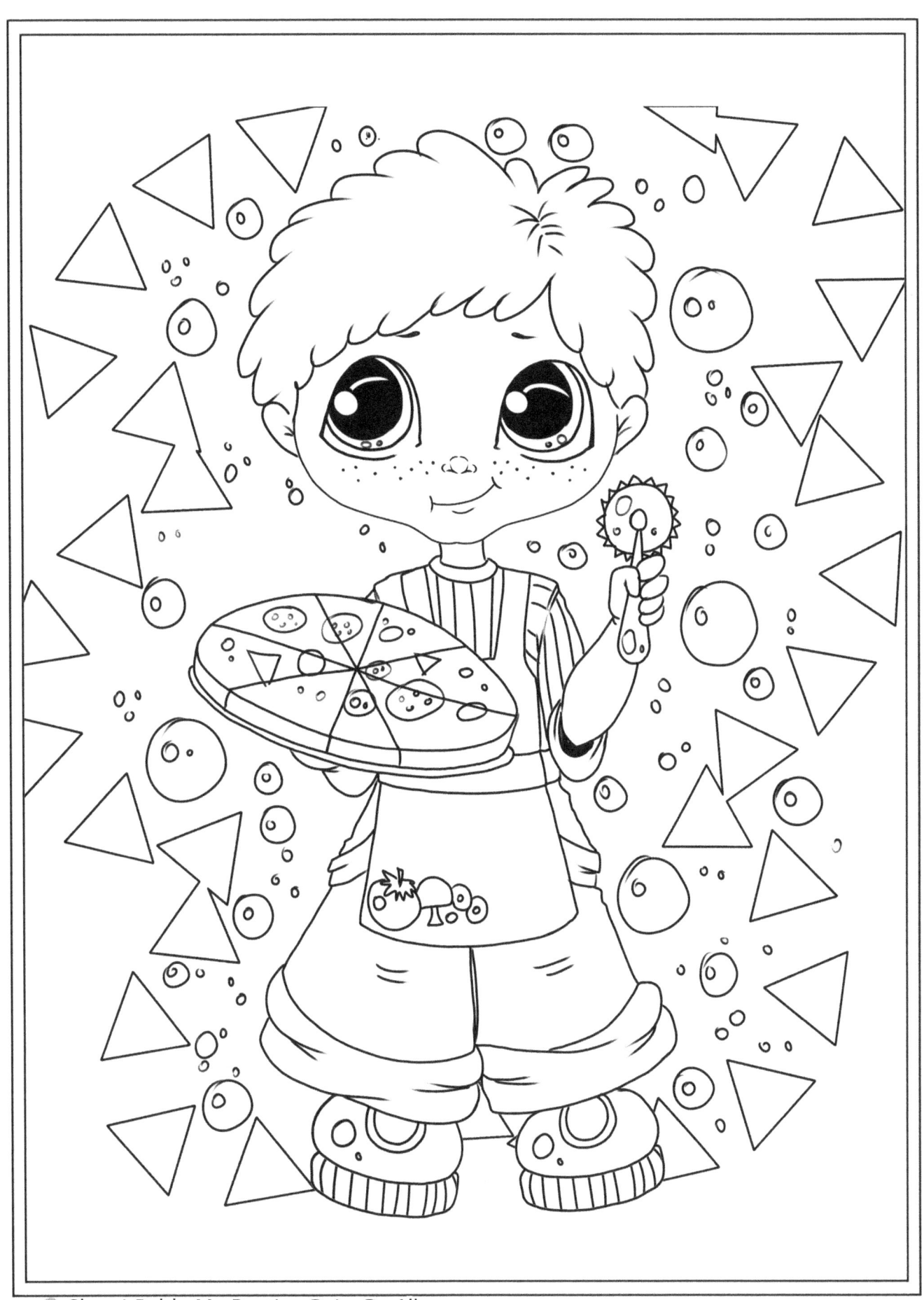

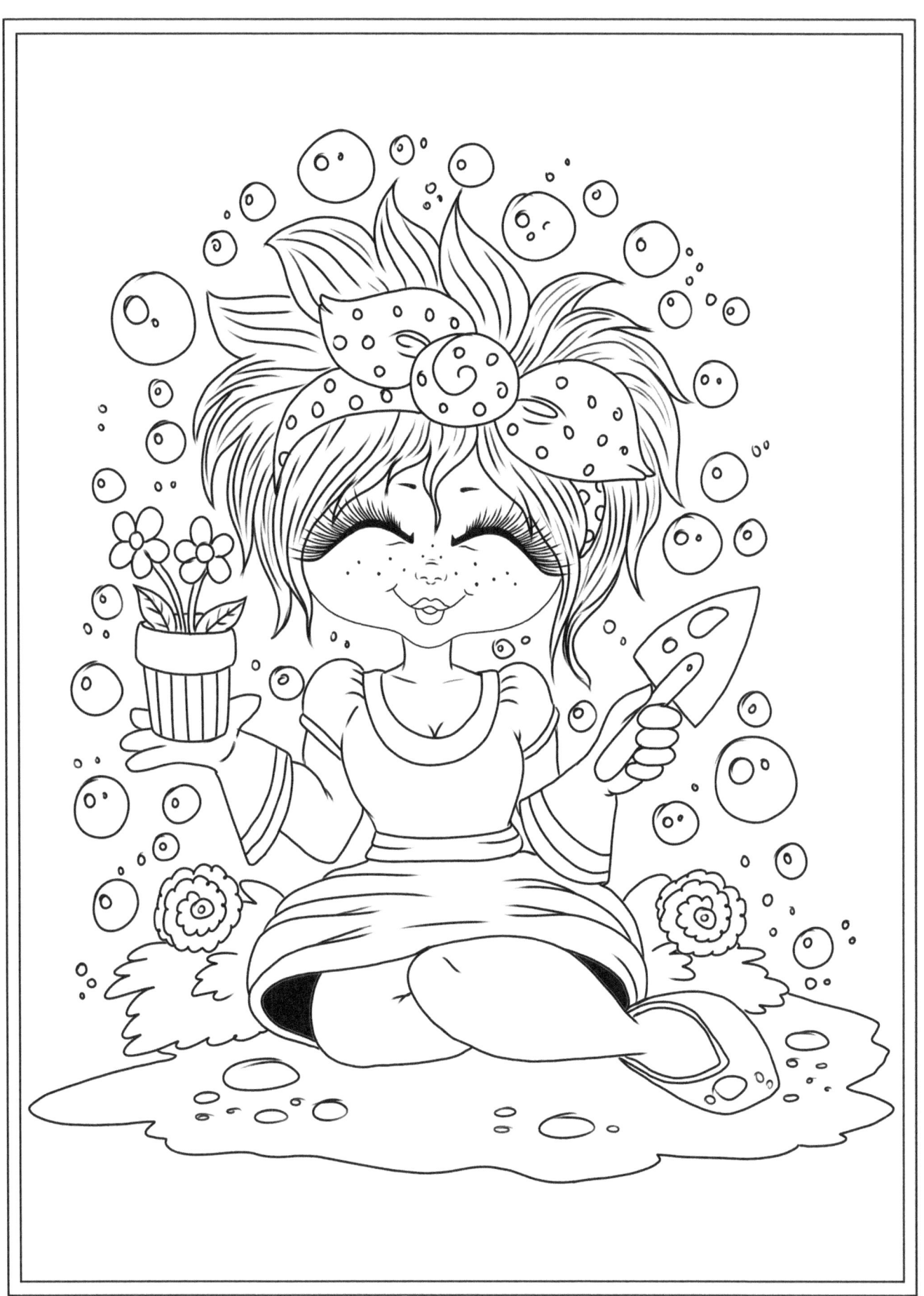

© Sherri Baldy My-Besties Daisy Do All

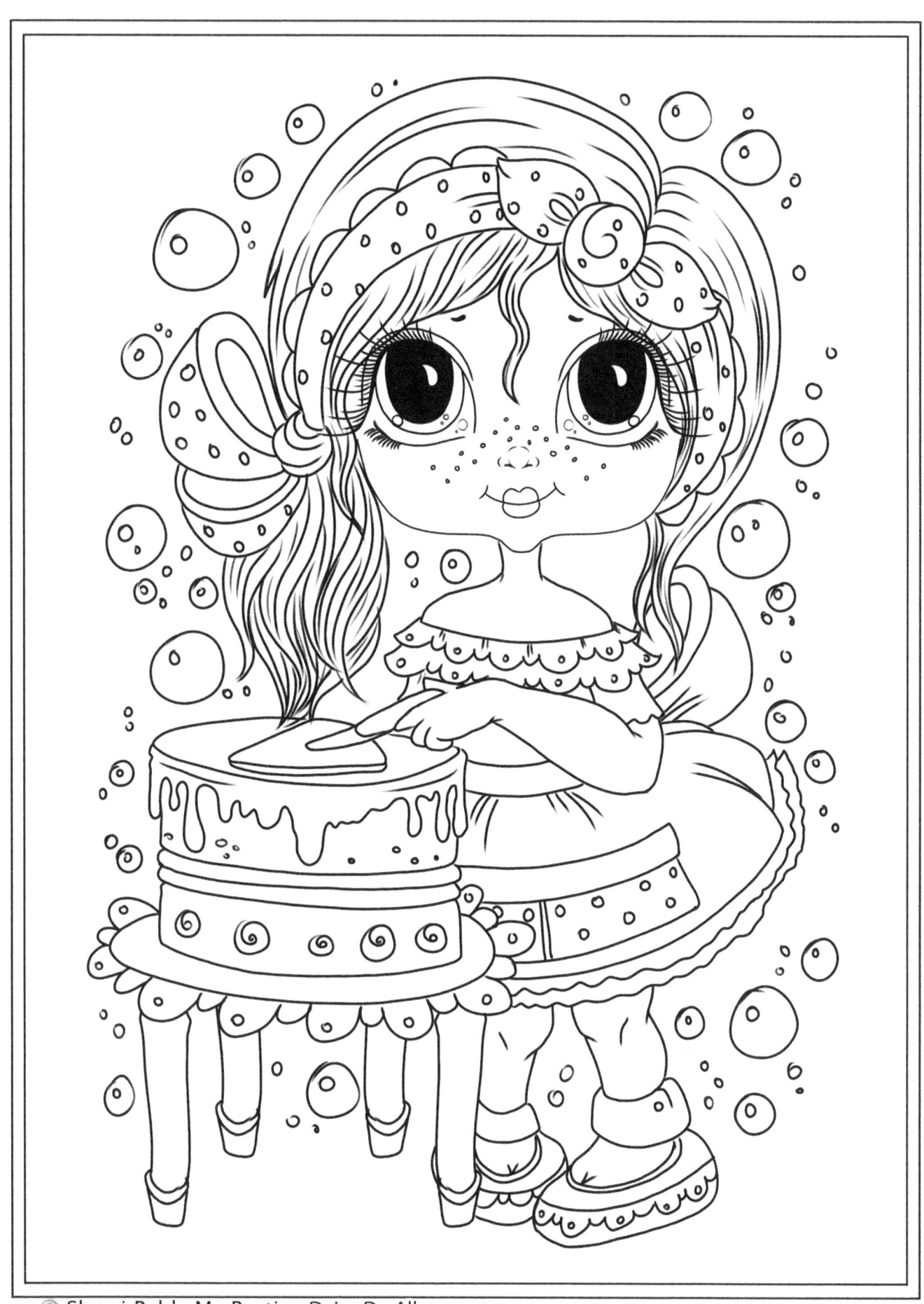

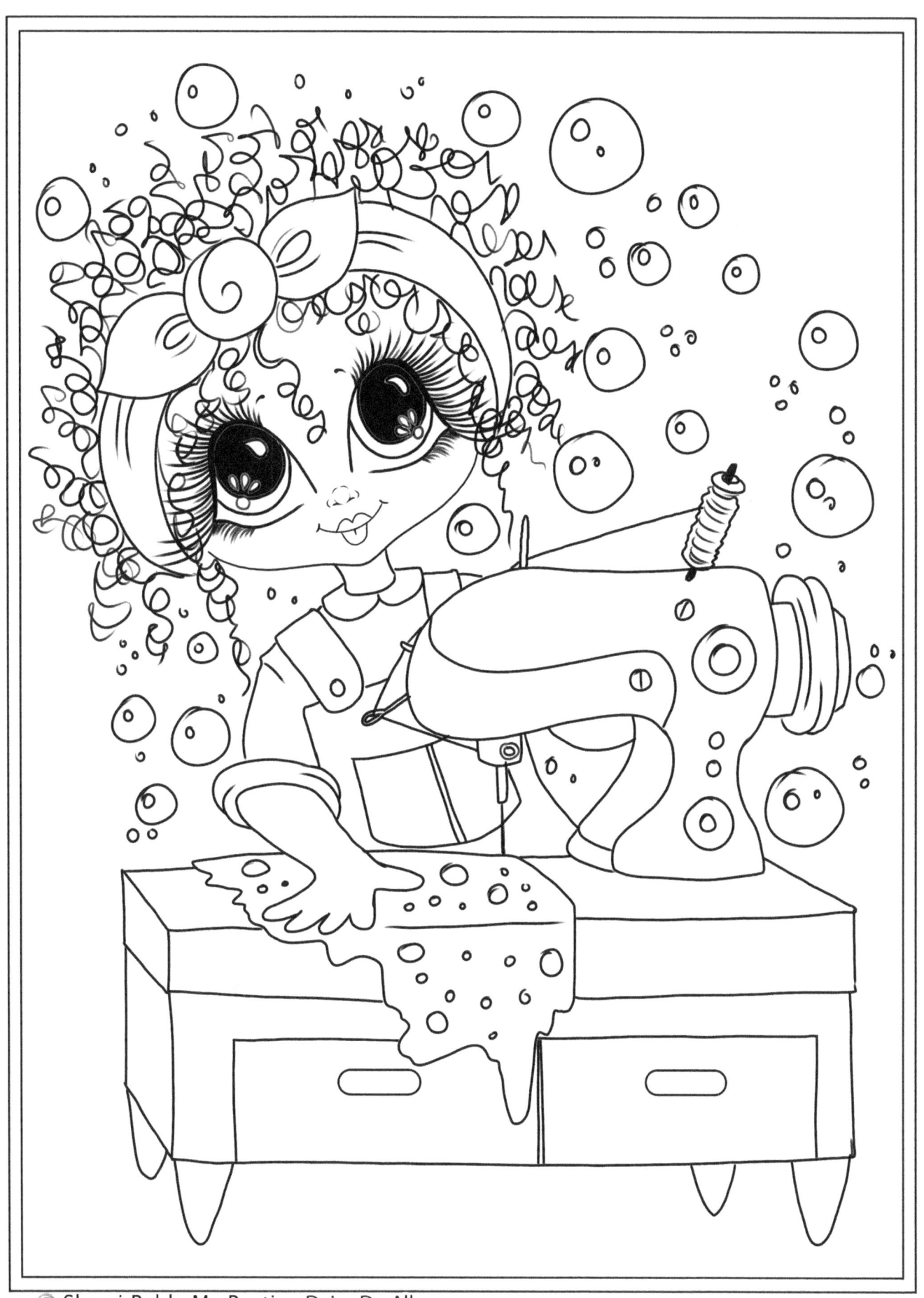

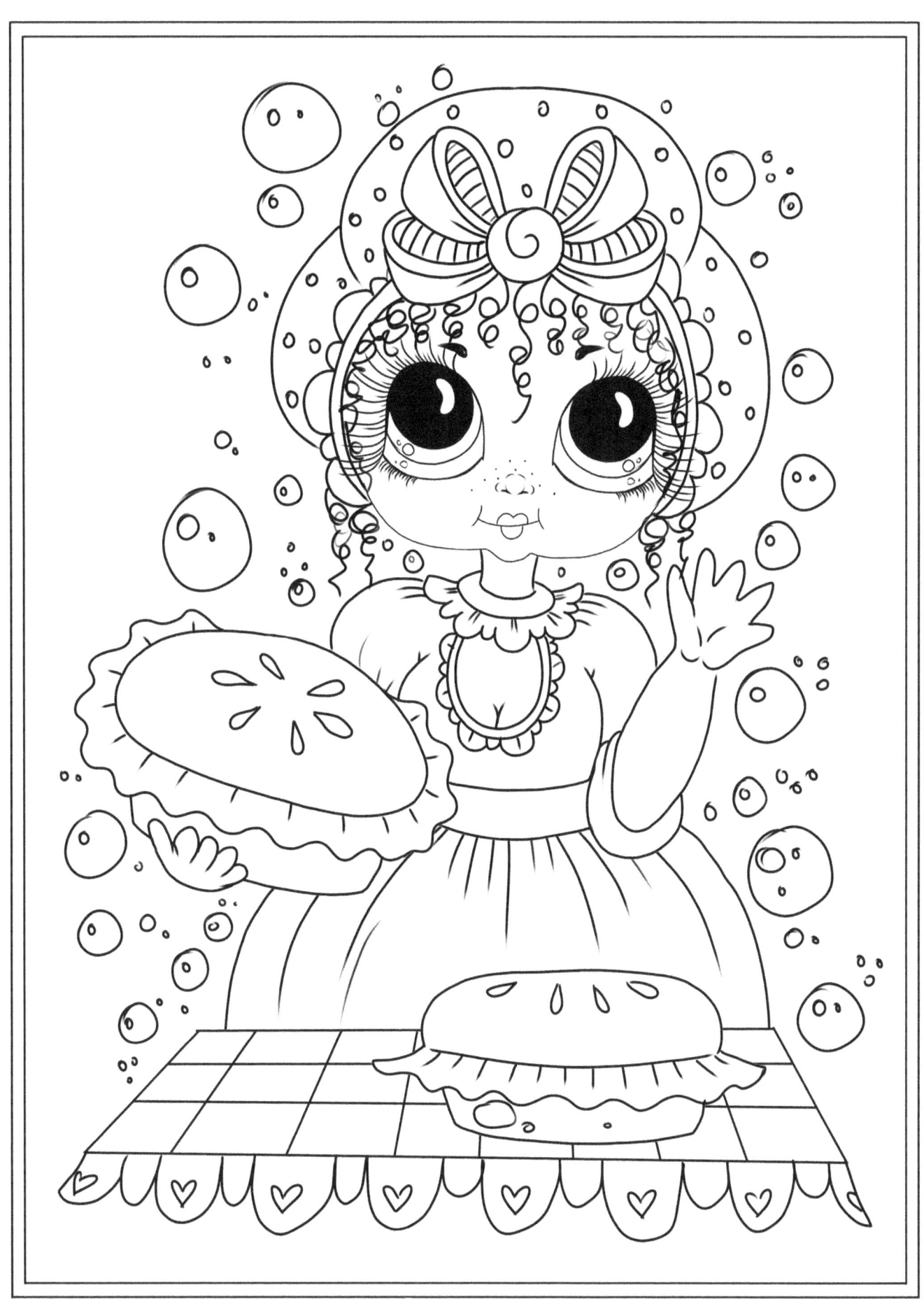

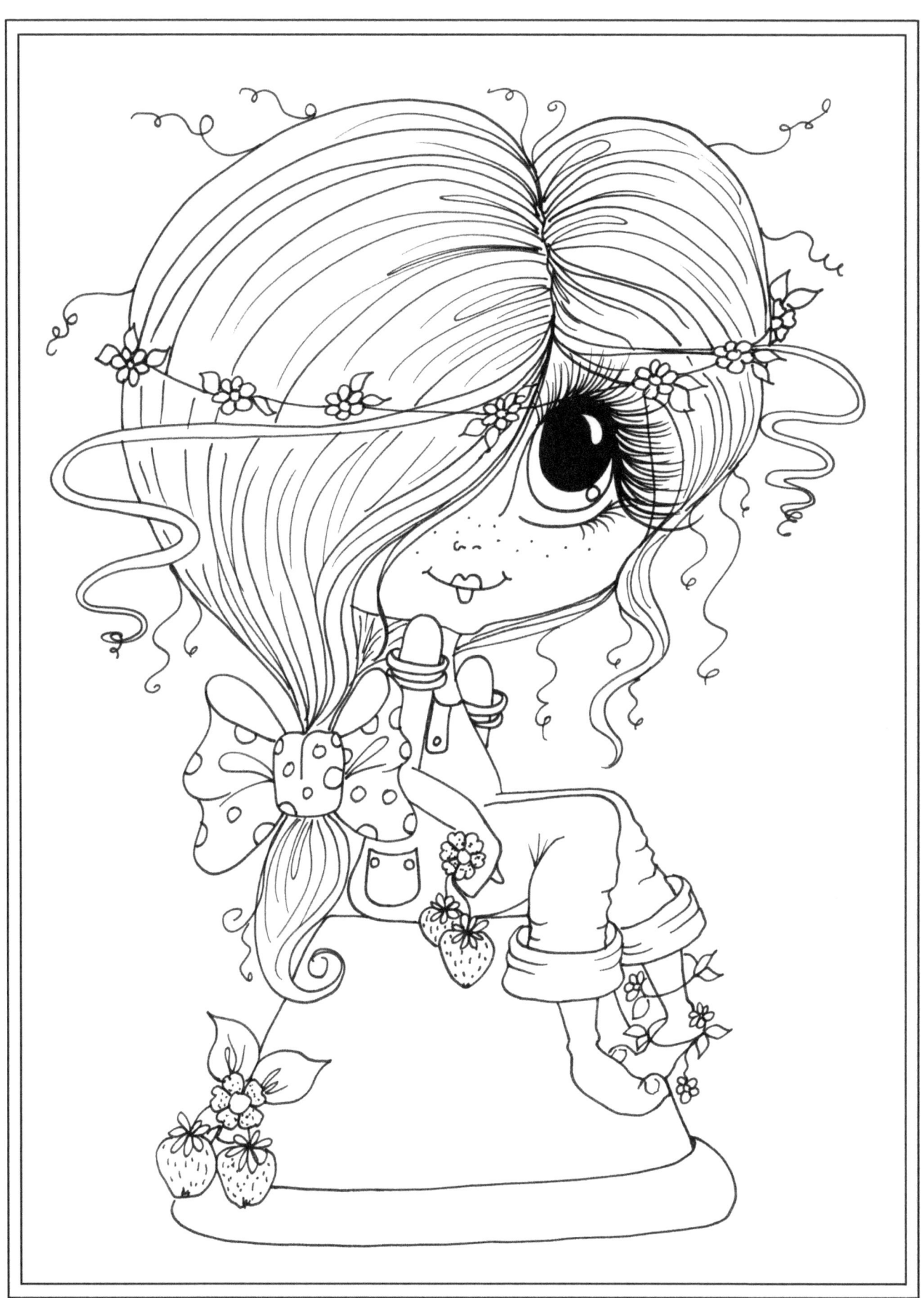

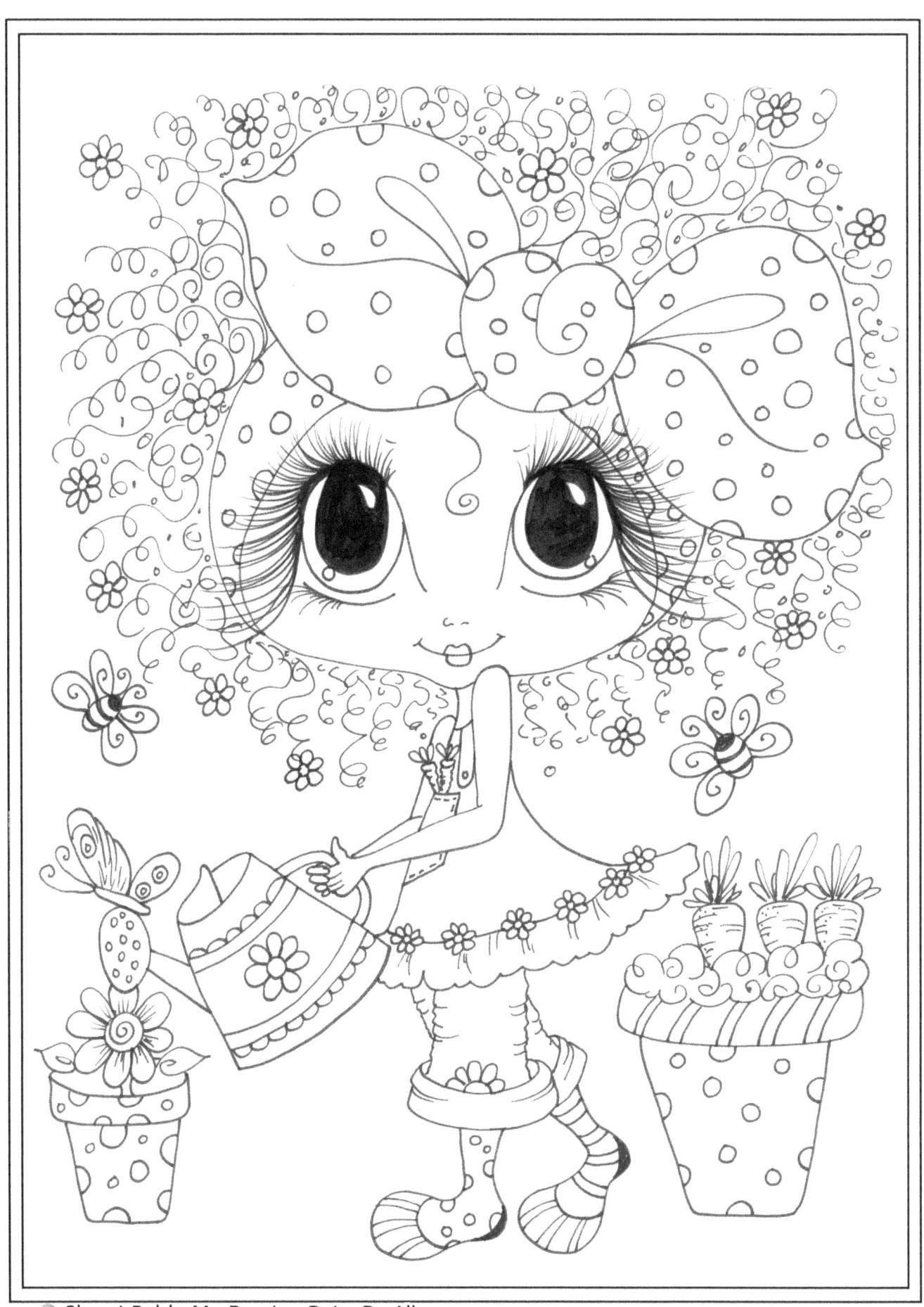

© Sherri Baldy My-Besties Daisy Do All

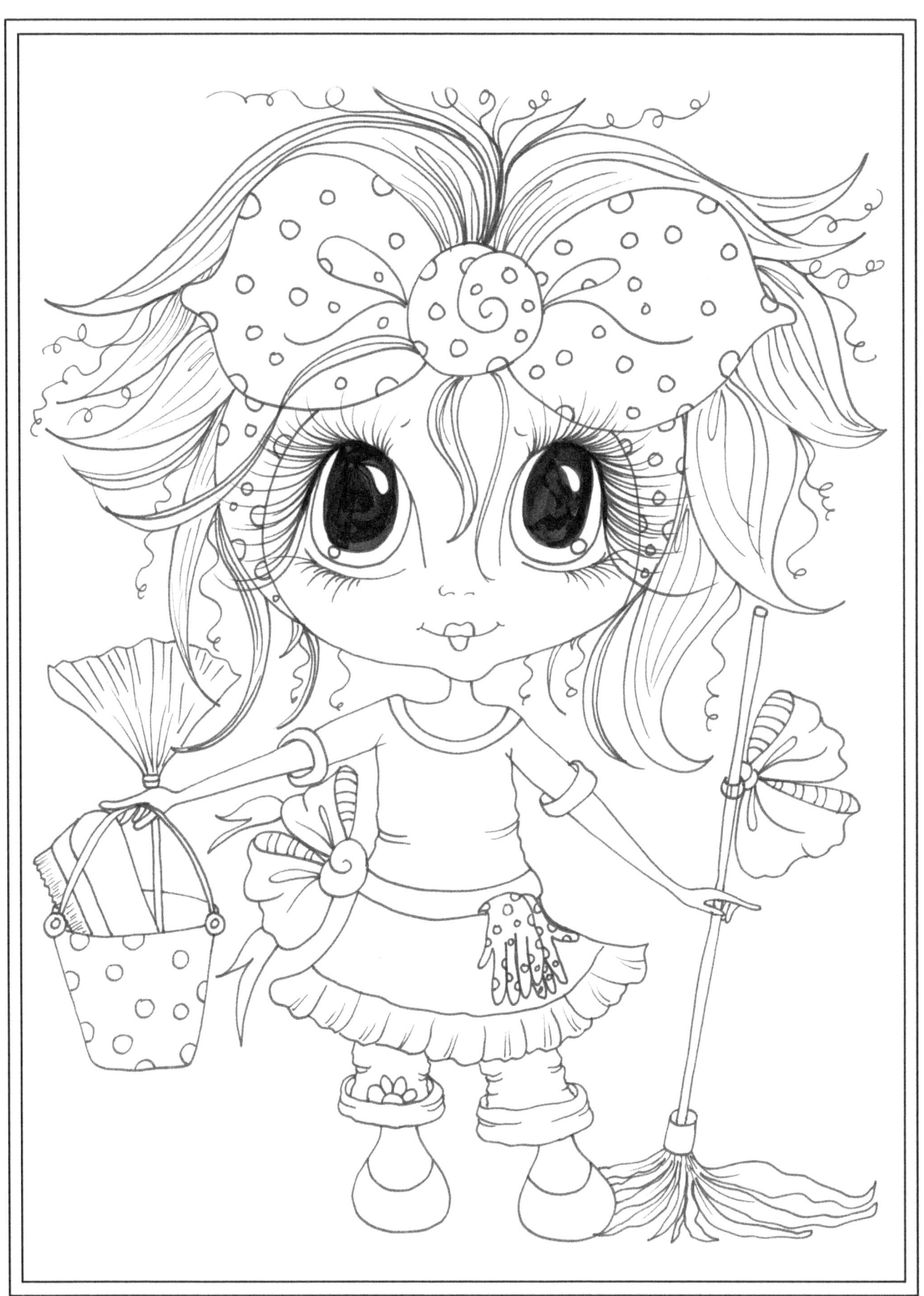

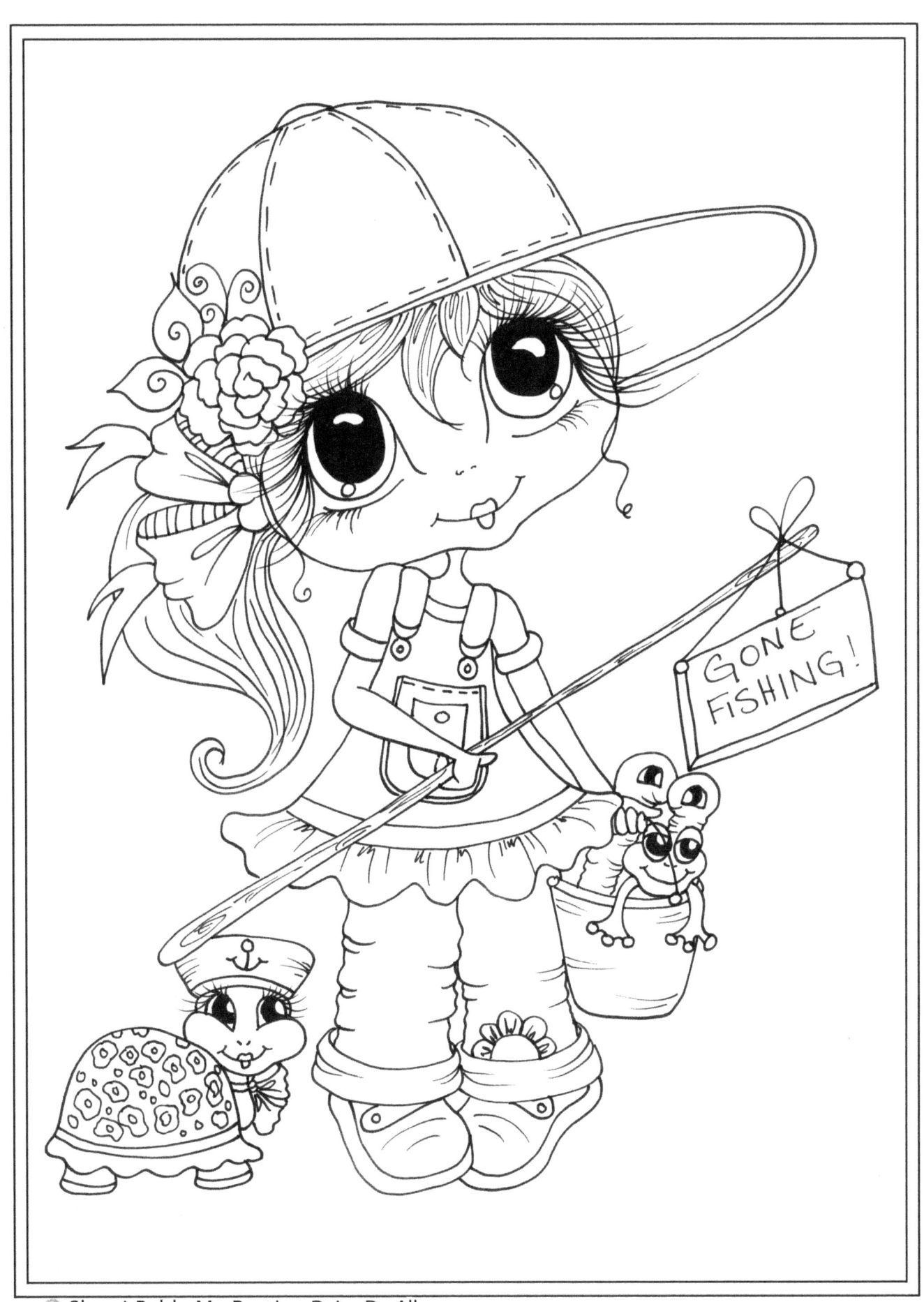

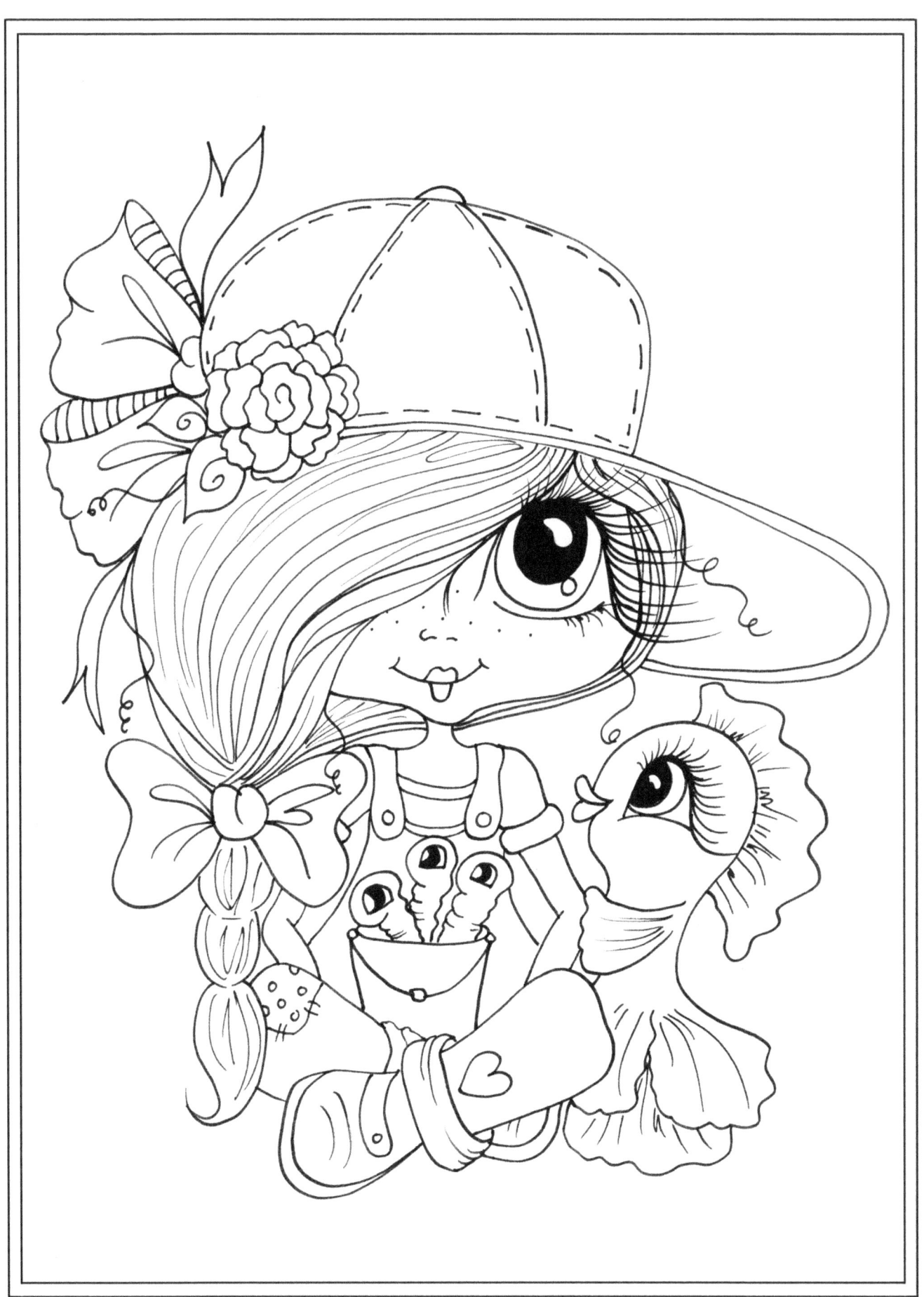

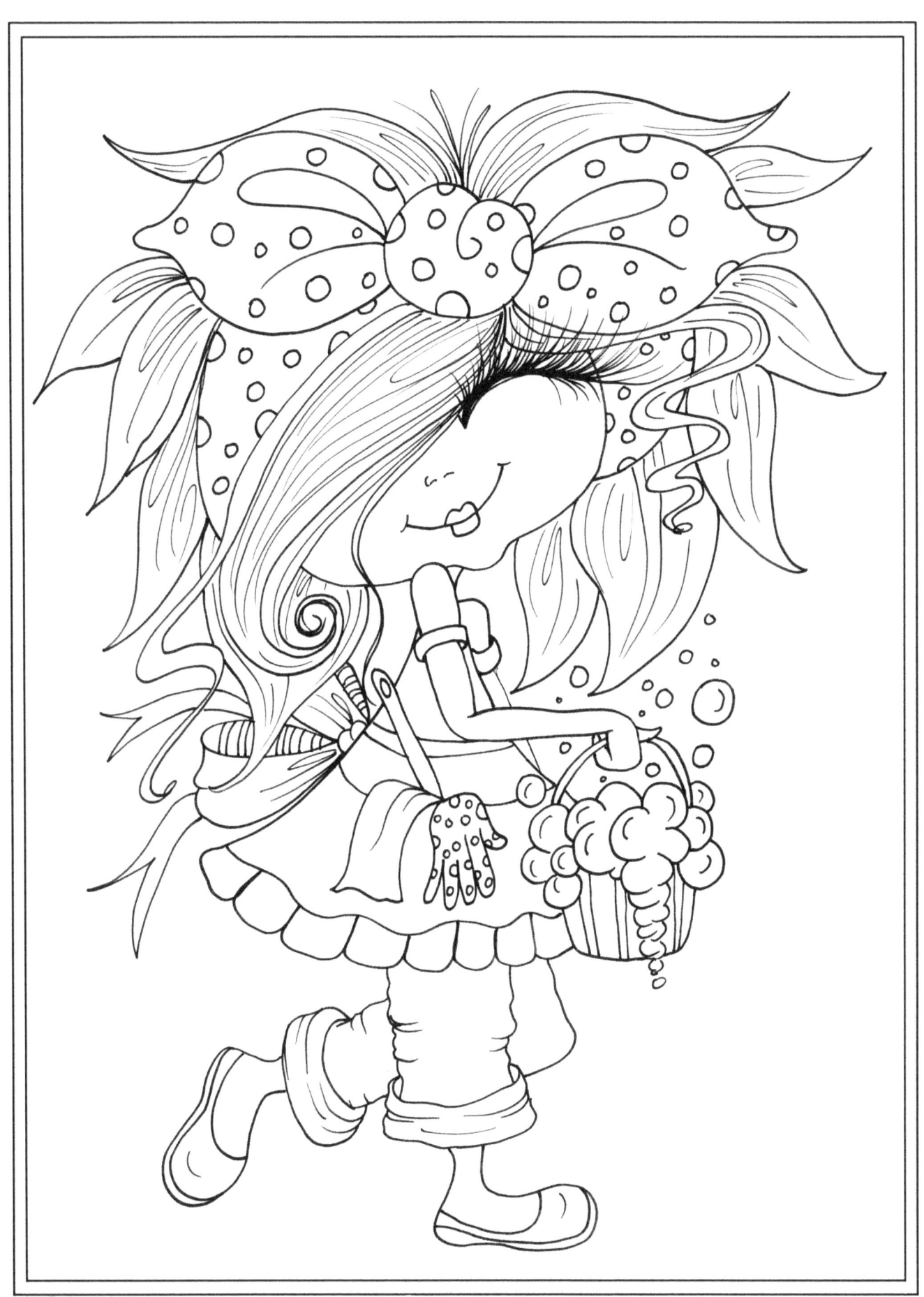

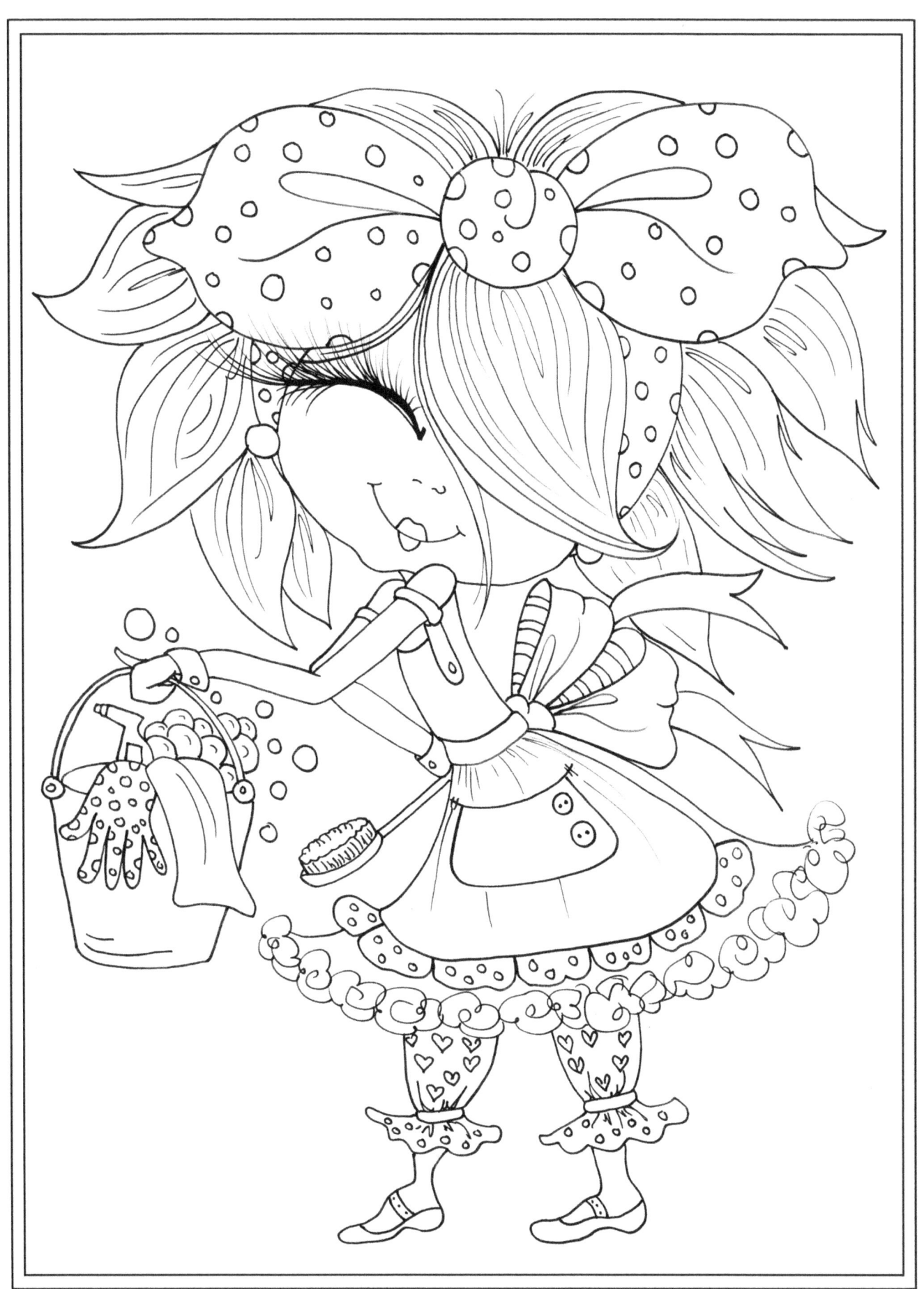

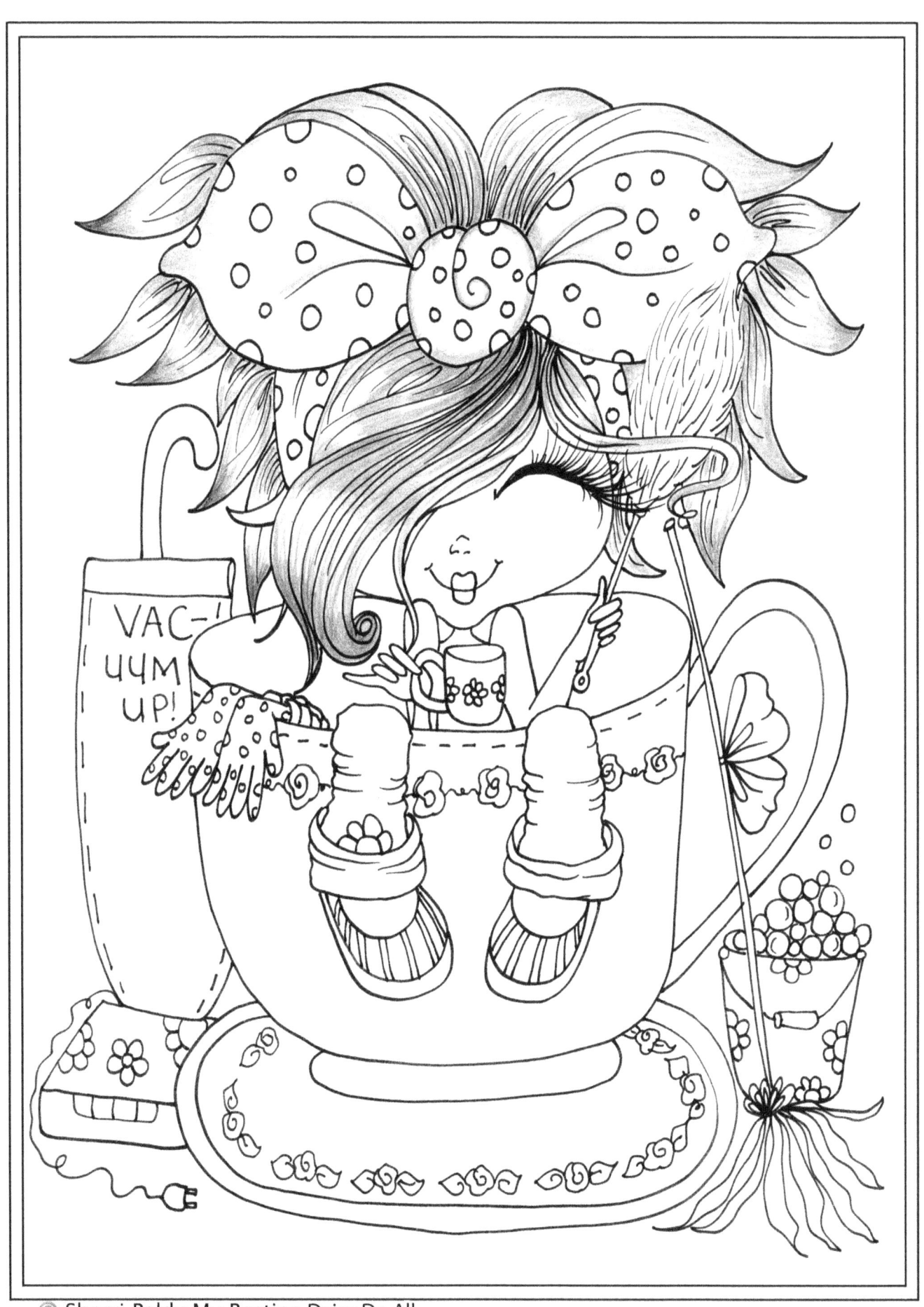

Coloring Books by Sherri Baldy

1. Gnome-Ville
2. Halloween Adorable Besties
3. Have a little Faith Besties
4. Fall Days
5. Flower Petal Pots
6. Fluffy's 1
7. Fluffy's 2
8. You drive me Batty
9. Spookylicious
10. Pinkles the Pink frog & Friends
11. I love Coffee
12. Adorable Blooms & Spring Things
13. My Besties Monsters Ever mini monsters
14. Lil Monsters 2
15. Alphabet Besties
16. Back to School
17. Christmas Cottage
18. Trick or Treat
19. Coloring Book Calendar & Birthstone Besties
20. Fairy Princess
21. Lil Rascals
22. Little Dimples
23. Little Rosie's Christmas
24. Flirty Fluffies
25. Magical Creatures & Enchanted PLaces
26. Magical Winter
27. Messy Bessy Jessy
28. Moon & Stars
29. Night before Christmas
30. Besties of Oz
31. Pets
32. Santa's Little Helpers
33. Some Bunny Loves you
34. Sweet heart
35. The magic of winter
36. Warm Christmas Nights
37. Birthday Coloring Book

Coloring Books by Sherri Baldy

Coming Soon:

Coloring Books by Sherri Baldy

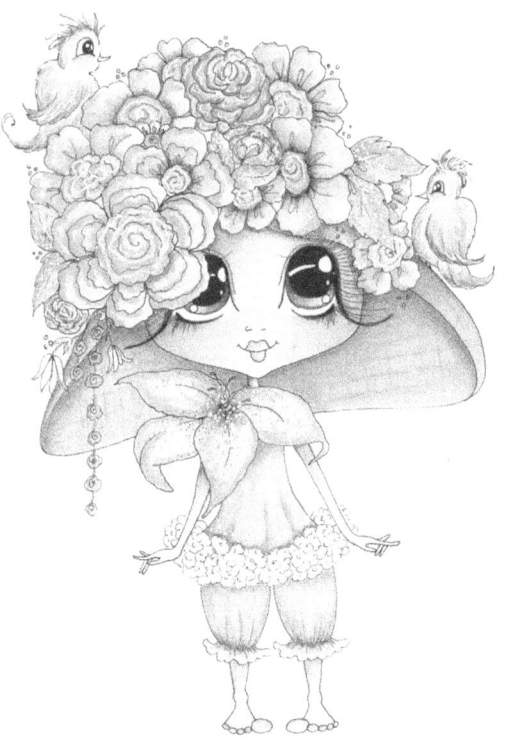

Color With Your Besties
Sherri Baldy
Coloring Books

Welcome to My Besties World!
Sherri invites you to come join in her SUPER
Friendly and FUN Crafting community!
We always look forward to seeing ALL the Sherri
Baldy My-Besties Creations by our coloring, crafter
friends from all around the world and We LOVE
meeting and making NEW Friends!
Come PARTY with us every few weeks at our FB
FUN NEW Releases where we have Loads of
Giveaways, Name Games going on and Freebies!!!
We share tips, tricks and techniques. Join in on the
FUN coloring & crafting group here:
https://www.facebook.com/groups/mybestiesdesign
s/
Our crafty group is a safe fun place for you to post
all your My Bestie Colorings, Creations, Photos,
Blog Posts, and More..... anything featuring our My
Besties Images, Stamps and Sherri Baldy Crafting
Products are welcome!
We have MANY Shops for you to enjoy featuring
Sherri Baldy My Bestie Craft Products!
Our My Bestie Shops:
www.MyBestiesShop.com
www.My-Besties.com
www.Scrapbookstampsociety.com

Our Etys Shop:
https://www.etsy.com/shop/SherriBaldy?ref=hdr_sh
op_menu

Join our Blog Challenges:

Our Sherri Baldy
Blog:http://sherribaldy.blogspot.com/

Sherri Baldy

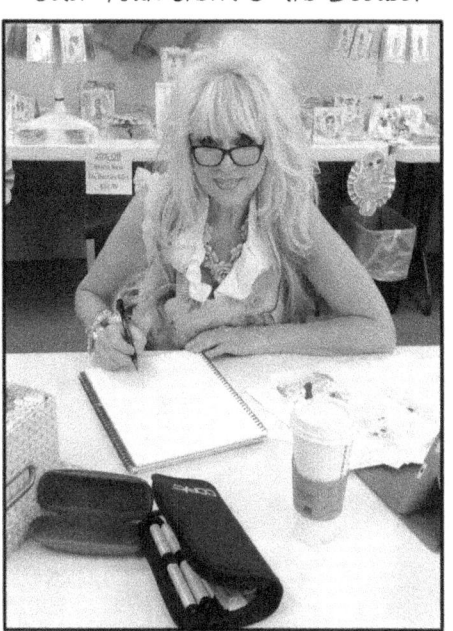

Color With Sherri & The Besties!

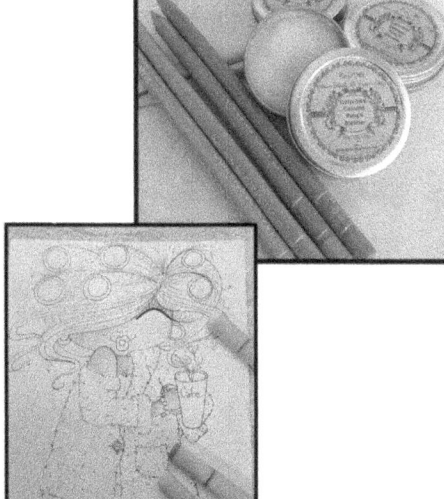

www.MyBestiesShop.com
Sherri Baldy My Besties Coloring Books in Riverside CA.
Copyright Sherri Baldy ~ My-Besties TM

www.ingramcontent.com/pod-product-compliance
Lightning Source LLC
Chambersburg PA
CBHW080820170526
45158CB00009B/2477